STREET CORNER UNIVERSITY

Memoirs of a Street Corner Kid

D. Holford

STREET CORNER UNIVERSE by D. Holford

Published by Street Corner Publications

© 2021 D. Holford

www.StreetCornerUniverse.com

ISBN: 978-0-578-83927-1

Original Cover Art by Susan Walsh McLean (Based on Design by D. Holford)

Book Cover Graphic Design by Juliana Gyimesi

Dedication

I would like to dedicate this book to several people:

First, to my wonderful wife, Laraine, for her ongoing love and support for all my endeavors, especially this one.

Next, to those with whom I shared the experiences you are about to read. For those of us who lived them in the 1960s, our block in Brooklyn was a universe—our universe—and the memories of those times will bind us together forever, regardless of time or space.

Also, to my children and grandchildren in the hopes that it will provide them with a glimpse of what life was like for me growing up. Despite changing circumstances over the generations, we all share the mutual joys and struggles that come from being young, experiencing new adventures, and trying to figure out things, as well as ourselves, along the way.

Finally, to all those who have stories to tell and books to write on whatever subject is burning in their hearts. While I have no illusions that the book you are about to read will win any Pulitzers, it is nonetheless the story that I have always wanted told.

It is in this spirit I now invite you all to share in the fun, silliness, and life-learning adventures I experienced growing up in my Street Corner Universe.

Love,
Donnie (aka Don, Dad, and Papa Don)

STREET CORNER UNIVERSE

Memoirs of a Street Corner Kid

Table of Contents

Introduction

The Street

WOODBINE STREET called to me like a life-altering beacon of acceptance and adventure during the formative years of my adolescence. Its distance of six blocks from my family's simple Brooklyn apartment provided a welcome sense of freedom and independence from the watchful eye of my mother and the shadow of my older brother. Often as I traveled there, I felt with each passing block a growing sense of excitement and anticipation about what new adventure lay in store once I arrived.

In contrast to the average city block, the one where we stayed was shorter in length, but not in accommodations. Up at the north end of Woodbine Street, running perpendicular to it, was Ridgewood Place. There, on the northwest corner, hummed a small knitting mill whose deep doorway provided excellent acoustics for hitting harmony on cold winter nights. On the opposing corner sat a cluster of single-car garages, against which we played handball and Ace-King-Queen, and on whose doors we scribbled heart-shaped updates on who was going out with whom—often crossed out by a subsequently aggrieved party.

Across the street from the garages loomed a large

lumberyard that stretched along Woodbine and the adjacent streets, insulating them from a busy shopping area on the other side. The lumberyard served as the home run boundary in stickball, two-and-a-half sewers from home plate but made longer by a fifteen-foot fence. For many, that chain-link monster stood as a defiant obstacle between the thrill of home run glory and the agony of a long out.

Irving Avenue intersected the south end of Woodbine. Its southwest corner hosted Bushwick High School, in whose gym we sought shelter on cold winter nights. Over on the opposite corner sat the Washington Irving branch of the public library, where we often engaged in passionate, whispered debates over whether Mickey Mantle could outhit Duke Snider or Willie Mays, and if the Dodgers could beat the Yankees in a World Series. These verbal exchanges sometimes lasted for hours, with each side citing countless statistics on home runs, batting averages, and stolen bases, whether relevant or not. In the end, most of us only wound up more firmly entrenched in our respective positions until some unexpected and innocent next time, when a casual remark might cause the debate to erupt all over again.

Midway on the block, two large elm trees stretched skyward from opposite sides of the street, leaning toward each other ever so slightly. Their entwined branches formed an arch of shade, providing welcome relief after long days of playing in the summer sun. They, as well as the younger trees scattered along both sides of the block, helped soften its "cityness" while also serving as first-down markers during winter games of touch football.

Along the sidewalks, assorted makes of parked automobiles rested patiently by the curbs. With the exception of Tuesdays and Thursdays, when there was alternate side parking, the '50s and early '60s models of Chevys, Pontiacs, and other car brands crouched bumper-to-bumper on both sides of the street. Their chrome grills and headlights resembled the faces of wild animals ready to roar off at a moment's notice.

And taking in the action from their front-row seats, the large-windowed houses appeared like giant spectators peering down on the arena below, where we played stickball or football by day and ring-a-lievio or other games at night. Huddled shoulder to shoulder on both sides of the street, most of the two- and three-family, cream-colored-brick buildings had their windowsills and doorways offset in fresh coats of brown or green enamel. Several tall gray six-family buildings also stood guard down near the Irving Avenue end.

All the houses were protected by black cast-iron picket fences, which demanded the utmost respect when we dared to scale them. Three-step concrete stoops greeted entrants into most every house, with short subterranean staircases underneath leading to secluded cellar doorways, where some of us learned and later faithfully practiced the age-old art of making out.

Perhaps to a stranger passing through, that block—*our* block—appeared no different than any other in Brooklyn during the 1960s. Yet to those of us who lived there, stayed there, and grew there, that street was a universe—*our* universe—full of wonderful, new, and lasting experiences. Though distant now, those days will always be recalled with warm smiles that lighten our faces, and their memories will bind forever those of us who shared them, regardless of time or space.

The following is the story of those experiences with—in

the words of *Dragnet*'s Joe Friday—the names changed to protect the innocent.

Chapter I

In the Beginning...

Lengthening daylight, blossoming trees, and warming breezes signaled an atmosphere of renewal in Brooklyn, New York, and launched the summer of 1962, a time of innocence filled with optimism and enthusiasm about the future.

John F. Kennedy was president, Robert Wagner was mayor, and New York had just welcomed a new baseball team, the Mets, to help us forget the Dodgers and Giants, who had deserted us five years earlier. I had already been in the Boy Scouts for a couple of years and had risen to the rank of Star, just two below Eagle. Each year, my troop sponsored a Parents' Night, an evening in which parents of the Scouts attended ceremonies where promotions, merit badges, and other awards were presented. Following the ceremonies, coffee and cake were served while Scouts performed short entertaining skits.

In preparation for that year's Parents' Night, two friends from my troop, Wally and Jeff, asked me to be in a skit they had written based on the old minstrel song "The Swanee River," made popular in the 1930s by Al Jolson. In our skit, a father and mother appeared in blackface, strolling their baby in a carriage while singing, "Swanee, Swanee, how I luvs ya, how I luvs ya, my dear ole Swanee."

At a designated point in the routine, the baby, complete with bonnet, bib, and bottle, was to poke his head through a crepe paper carriage top and sing out, "Wish I was in the land of cotton, ole times there are not forgotten, look away, look away, look away, Dixie Land!"

(While this might appear so politically incorrect by today's standards, please bear in mind that it was 1962, and our intention was innocent humor, not racial insensitivity.)

Wally, who weighed over three hundred pounds, played the father; Jeff, who weighed over two hundred pounds, played the mother; and yours truly, weighing in at one hundred ten pounds soaking wet, played the baby. In addition to being one of the few in my troop who could fit into the carriage, I was probably the only one dumb enough to be talked into doing it.

As Parents' Night approached, we spent more and more time at Wally's house, rehearsing the skit and putting some finishing touches on an old baby carriage we had found. Following the recent divorce of his parents, Wally, along with his father, had moved in with an aunt and uncle who lived on Woodbine Street. He'd only briefly met some local kids but didn't know any of them very well.

One day, after rehearsing for a few hours, we took a break on Wally's stoop. His house, located near the middle of the block, was one of the few with a high stoop. It provided a panoramic view of the street below, where a stickball game was in progress. As we watched the game, Jeff commented that the distance needed to hit a home run over the fence of the lumberyard up the block didn't appear to be very far. Wally and I both agreed, and then Wally, in a loud and booming voice, took the liberty of communicating this observation in a less-than-diplomatic manner to the players down on the field.

"Hey, you guys must be a bunch of punks if you can't hit it over that fence. I've got a six-year-old sister who could do it left-handed!"

"Punk" was a popular rank word frequently bestowed without regard or understanding of its true meaning.

"Hey, fat boy," a voice from the street responded, "if your sister is as big and ugly as you, you could probably bounce the ball off her stomach, and it would go over the fence. You're so fat, you'd be lucky if you could even swing a bat!"

The Peace Corps this wasn't.

Not one to beat around the bush, Wally swiftly shifted the exchange from words to action. "Well, if you're so sure I can't swing a bat, why don't we play a game to find out? Me and my two friends will play any four of you guys and still whip your asses!"

In a matter of seconds, Jeff and I found ourselves swept up in Wally's challenge against the kids on the street, who at first appeared reluctant to stop their game. However, after a brief discussion, they accepted the challenge, undoubtedly tempted by their favorable odds and the opportunity to shut Wally up.

Stickball teams usually consisted of three players, but Wally was giving them the chance to have a fourth fielder who could play on the sidewalk and chase foul pops that might otherwise be unreachable. It was too tempting for them to pass up.

Several games and hours later, the wins and losses were almost evenly divided. While a home run had looked easy from Wally's stoop, the upward incline of the block, combined with the lumberyard's tall chain-link fence, made hitting a home run much more difficult than we'd initially thought. While none of us hit any home runs, we did get a chance to meet the kids we played against, all of whom either lived or hung out on the block.

Their outfielder was a Chinese kid named Richie. His parents owned a Chinese restaurant around the corner, and he was sometimes called "Leechie" by the others. The second baseman was Timmy, a slender German lefty who resembled a young blond Steve Allen, with the same quick sense of humor. Playing the infield was Ralphie, a soft-spoken, short, freckled Irish kid, well-liked by the crowd and perhaps the best fielding player on their team. The fourth member of their team was a dark-haired, heavy-browed Italian kid named Mario, also known as M.C., whose grandfather had threatened to "choppa our hands off" during the games if we hit any windows on his house.

At the conclusion of the final inning, we took time out to discuss the game's highlights. When the play-by-play reviews ended, the kids from the block went home to eat lunch, and Wally, Jeff, and I went to get sodas and Devil Dogs before returning to Wally's stoop. The soda companies had just introduced sixteen-ounce bottles, and after a few games of stickball in the midday sun, it seemed like that much soda wouldn't quench our thirsts. As always, though, our eyes were bigger than our stomachs, and around thirteen ounces of the way through, we felt like we were about to explode.

After sitting on the stoop for a while and talking about the lumberyard fence, we noticed a slender brown-haired girl dressed in a yellow print blouse, solid yellow shorts, and white tennis sneakers come bouncing out of a house a few doors down on our side of the street. As she passed us, I felt compelled to say something, but the best I could come up with was, "Hi there."

She responded with a slight smile, then hurried up the block toward Ridgewood Place, where she turned the corner and disappeared.

No sooner was she out of sight than I turned to Wally and asked, "Who's that?"

"Her name is Ellen or something like that," he responded. "She's Italian and lives in the house she just came out of."

"I think I like her," I said.

In those days, it was quick and easy to know if you liked someone. If you liked the way they looked, that was usually all that mattered, especially for me since I didn't have a whole lot of experience to go by.

No sooner had I told Wally that I liked the girl when an identical one came bopping out of the same house in the same manner, also disappearing up the block.

As I watched her pass, I didn't say anything, but I did do a double take.

Wally laughed. "No, you're not seeing things. This one's name is Colleen, although maybe the other one is Colleen and this one is Ellen."

A jingle from the popular Doublemint gum television commercial immediately formed on my lips.

"Double your pleasure," I whispered.

"Double your fun," he finished.

To me, the Twins' names didn't matter, and I began to smile. In a few short minutes, the odds of meeting the girl I had decided I liked had already doubled!

During the next few days, further investigation revealed that one twin was named Eileen, not Ellen, and from up close, the Twins—whom I always thought of with a capital T—could be told apart. Eileen usually wore serious facial expressions, while Colleen was always eating something, though her ninety-eight-pound body never showed it.

Knowing Eileen's name was only the first of many steps that had to be taken before I officially introduced myself. Approaching someone you liked was a serious matter and had to be done carefully, after much planning. While a certain amount of admiring might take place from a safe distance, no direct encounter would be attempted until the proper groundwork had been laid. This included plotting how and where the first contact would take place, figuring out what to say and how to respond if she said this or that, and finally deciding what the next step would be if all the figuring succeeded—or worse, if it failed. While some time passed before I actually spoke to Eileen, this minor detail did not get in the way of word spreading that "Danny liked Eileen."

The fact that I, Danny, had not so much as spoken two words to Eileen was irrelevant.

Another girl on the block, Lisa, was also Italian. In contrast to the Twins, who were, to put it mildly, skinny, Lisa was short and much heavier. Although Lisa was prettier than the Twins and had a more outgoing personality, her weight was a drawback. For a twelve-year-old boy with virtually no experience with girls, physical features were by far the most important criteria in determining a girl's attractiveness.

Personality counted about one percent.

Together, the Twins and Lisa comprised the main female contingent of our crowd. While there were other girls on the block who wanted to be included, they were younger and regarded as mere children by those of us who saw ourselves as older and more mature.

The last member of the Woodbine Street crowd, whom I

had yet to meet, was a guy named Pete. Based on the way the others referred to him, he was the leader of the pack and also my biggest competition for Eileen's attention—because word was out that she liked him.

A few nights after I first spotted Eileen, a stickball game was arranged. It was now well into summer, and it didn't get dark until late, though I still had to be home by eight thirty. Rumor had it that the mystery guy, Pete, was going to play, so at least I'd finally get a chance to meet him.

Upon my arrival, as I turned the corner of the block and headed toward Wally's house to pick him up, someone called out.

"Hey, Danny!"

I turned and saw a short, dark-skinned Italian kid sitting on a parked car with a stickball bat in his hands. I looked at him more closely as I approached. Something about him looked familiar, but I couldn't place him.

He hopped off the car and came over to me, extending his hand. "Hi, Danny, I'm Pete."

He acted as though he knew me, yet I didn't remember him.

"Guess you don't remember me," he said, apparently seeing the blank stare on my face.

"Can't say that I do."

"A few summers ago, I played at the schoolyard down the block from where you live. We played against each other a few times in punchball."

I struggled for a minute and then remembered. Back then, he'd been short for his age and sometimes got bullied by bigger but younger kids. *Could this be the same Pete that Eileen liked?* From all indications, he was.

11

"Yes, now I remember," I said. "You seem much older since then."

While waiting for Wally to come out, Pete and I got into a game of Pitching In, with Jeff serving as the official catcher. In the third inning, Pete was at bat, and I had pitched myself into a jam by walking him three times to load the bases. I couldn't walk him again without scoring a run, so I thought back to the old days in the schoolyard and felt that maybe I could just lay one over. I wound up and lobbed him a pitch that had MEATBALL written all over it. As the ball neared the plate, Pete took a full swing, smashing not only the ball but my old memories of him as well.

I can't remember who won the game that night, but I'll never forget the feeling I had about all the new kids I had met on the block. They had warmly accepted me for myself, not because I was someone else's kid brother or because I had gotten good grades in school.

A couple of days later, Wally, Jeff, and I performed our skit, and it was a big hit. By then, however, it had become very clear to me that I had found something much more important than merit badges.

I had finally found a crowd of my own.

Chapter II

Religious Instructions

After I'd spent a few days with the Woodbine Street crowd, Pete invited me to join them to attend Sunday Mass. I felt honored, as though the invitation was another sign of my acceptance into the crowd.

I usually went to Sunday Mass at St. Barbara's, the church where I received my First Holy Communion and was later confirmed—two painfully unforgettable religious experiences of my life. I attended elementary school at P.S. 116, an old public school conveniently located down the block from where I lived. Unlike my friends who went to parochial school, I had to attend religious instruction when it was time for me to receive First Holy Communion and Confirmation. I went on Wednesday afternoons via early release from school and then again on Sundays, immediately following the 8:00 a.m. Mass, known as the early-bird special.

The two primary teaching tools used by the nuns at the time were fear and intimidation, supplemented with healthy doses of corporal punishment. At the beginning of our weekly catechism lessons, the public-school kids were often treated to nonstop propaganda about how attending parochial school would make us less likely to fall prey to Communism.

When the opening infomercials concluded at each of our

13

First Holy Communion classes, we were treated to graphic visuals depicting how our souls were like white sheets of silk that became dirtied with black stains when we committed a sin.

The stains could be caused by two types of sins: mortal and venial. Venial sins, resulting from the use of profanity like "damn" or "shit," were less serious and could be easily removed in confession with a sincere act of contrition followed by penance of a few Hail Marys or Our Fathers. In the unfortunate event that one died with a venial sin on their soul before getting to confession, the price to pay was a time-limited stay in purgatory, an unpleasant place that was hot as hell. However, after a few decades in purgatory reflecting and repenting, the soul could enter heaven.

In contrast to venial sins, the mortal ones were much more serious and involved offenses such as missing Mass, stealing, looking at "dirty" pictures, or having "impure" thoughts for prolonged periods of time. The stains caused by mortal sins required much stronger spiritual detergent, involving longer stays of admonition in the confessional booth, a stern lecture from the priest, and the harsher penance of saying the Rosary. If one had the misfortune of dying with a mortal sin on their soul, the consequence was spending all eternity in the fires of hell.

For public-school kids, classroom punishment was often supplemented by additional doses of fear and intimidation at the 8:00 a.m. Mass on Sundays. Catholic-school kids got to sit in smaller groups of six in the pews located near the front of the church, closer to the altar and the priest. We public-school kids, on the other hand, were herded into groups of eight or ten in rear pews, adjacent to sculptures graphically depicting tortured souls in purgatory, desperately reaching toward heaven.

While the Catholic-school kids went unguarded, we were constantly patrolled by nuns with clickers, who signaled to us inferior beings when to kneel, sit, or stand. Any of us unlucky enough to get caught whispering or napping during Mass were pulled out of the pew, usually by our ears, and marched to the rear vestibule like lambs being led to slaughter out of eyewitness range. When the victims returned, red handprints could be seen on one cheek or the other, a scarlet reminder to remain awake and silent in God's house.

By the time we attended religious instruction for Confirmation, we hypothesized that the names of the nuns (they always had two male first names) were code for whatever torture treatment they specialized in. Those of us who had Sister Dennis Patrick, aka D.P., were convinced that D.P. really stood for Deadly Pincher, one of her favorite methods for administering punishment.

In addition to pinching, Sister D.P. also utilized experiential learning as a teaching aid. As such, her classroom's six rows of desks were organized into two rows each of heaven, purgatory, and hell. The two rows in heaven were near the open front door of the room, accessible to cool fresh air from the hallway. The two hell rows were near the far wall, adjacent to three large cast-iron radiators that emitted exorbitant amounts of heat throughout the year.

At the beginning of the year, as in life, we all started in heaven, and each week we had to memorize several questions and answers from our *Baltimore Catechism*. If we got the answers correct, we stayed in heaven; however, if we failed to accurately recite any of the assigned questions and answers, we were banished to hell. At the next class, if those of us banished to hell recited the assigned questions and answers correctly, we were moved to purgatory. If we accurately recited the questions and answers again the following week, we got to ascend back into heaven. Thus, through this simple experiential process, Sister D.P. instilled in us the lifelong lesson that the fall from grace was easy, but the journey back to redemption was much more difficult.

After all the religious instruction ended, I found that attending Sunday Mass was a necessary but not necessarily pleasant experience. At the time, Mass was still said in Latin, and between the heat of the summer and not understanding a single thing that was going on, the forty-minute Mass seemed more like forty days. In summer, the only relief from the heat came from the large fans in the front of the church, which did little more than blow hot air around while making an annoying humming sound. As a result, most people arrived early to sit near the altar, not because of the religious significance but because that's where the fans were.

However, once I met the Woodbine Street crowd, Sunday Mass took on a new meaning. Usually, the crowd went to the ten o'clock Mass at St. Brigid's, a church that was physically closer to my house but not considered my parish because of some crazy church zoning rules. There were two ten o'clock Masses at St. Brigid's: the High Mass upstairs in the church and the Low Mass in the basement chapel. The High Mass was the full-blown production, complete with choir singing, organ music, benediction, and long sermons. The Low Mass we attended was much less formal and, more importantly, fifteen minutes shorter.

The Catholic members of the crowd—Pete, the Twins,

Lisa, M.C., and I—agreed to meet at a quarter to ten in front of the six-family house where Pete and the Twins lived. Neither Timmy nor Richie were Catholic, and Ralphie was an altar boy who had to serve Mass at different times.

The first time I met the crowd, I tried my best to impress Eileen. When I asked my older brother for advice, he responded, "Remember what the Gillette razor blade commercial says: Look Sharp! Be Sharp!"

Since my brother always had luck with girls, I took his advice and wore a green sharkskin suit I had gotten the Easter before. I felt I looked really "boss" in my suit, dress shirt, and best tie, with my hair slicked back by half a jar of Vaseline. However, as soon as I turned the corner onto the block, I felt out of place; everyone else had worn casual clothes.

"Hey, look at Danny all dressed up," M.C. shouted as soon as he saw me. "Between the green suit and his bright red hair, he could pass for a traffic light!"

We all had a good laugh, and I quickly realized that what had proved successful for my brother was not necessarily going to work for me.

As we started for church, I noticed that Eileen looked incredibly sad. I tried to start a conversation with her, but she walked on ahead and barely responded. Finally, I asked Pete what was going on.

"Oh, nothing, Dan," he said. "I guess she doesn't feel like talking."

I was concerned that it might have something to do with me, so I pressed him. "You sure? She's acting as though I did something to her. I tried to talk to her, but she barely spoke to me, and then she walked away."

"Don't worry. Whatever it is, she'll get over it. Just give

her some time."

Halfway to church, Lisa, acting as an intermediary for Eileen, waited for us, letting Eileen remain in front by herself.

"Danny," Lisa said, "can I talk to you a minute?"

"Sure, what's up?"

"Did you know that Eileen was going out with Pete?"

"No. How would I know that?"

"Well, she is—that is, *was*—until a few days ago when Pete broke up with her. He wanted to give her a chance to see if she liked you since he knows you like her."

"I had no idea they were going out. How come Pete never mentioned it to me?"

"He didn't want anyone to know. Eileen only told me after he broke up with her. She thinks you're a nice guy, but she really likes Pete and wants to go back with him. I thought I should let you know so you don't waste your time barking up the wrong tree, and because I'd like to see them get back together."

After our conversation, I caught up with Pete. He'd been walking with M.C., who dropped back to talk to Colleen and Lisa when I approached.

"Pete, I just found out from Lisa that you and Eileen were going out. How come you never mentioned anything?"

"Well, when you told me how much you liked her, I felt kind of bad telling you that she and I were going out. I wanted to keep our relationship quiet because I didn't want anyone to know, especially Colleen."

"Why didn't you want Colleen to know? They're sisters."

Pete elaborated on the complexities of the situation. "That's precisely the reason, Dan! You see, I was going out with Eileen, but I also like Colleen. If I just break up with Eileen and then go out with Colleen, there's bound to be hard feelings between them. The easiest way to break up with someone is to start an argument with them. That's what I did with Eileen. Now she wants to get back with me, but I want to give her time to see if she likes you, since I know you dig her. In the meantime, I want to check out how I feel about Colleen. Got it?"

"I think so," I said, not sure if he was doing me a favor.

At the completion of our busy journey, we arrived at church just as Mass was about to begin. Upon entering the basement chapel, I started for the front. Pete grabbed my arm and ushered me to a rear pew to join him and the others. Recalling my experience getting close to the fans, I asked him why we were sitting in the back.

"Just trust me," he said. "You'll see more from back here."

Every few seconds or so, the door behind us squeaked open, and people tiptoed past us as they headed up the aisle. The front door was located near the pulpit, so latecomers sneaked in through the back door to avoid admonishing glances from the priest. With the Twins and Lisa standing or kneeling reverently in the pew in front of us, M.C., Pete, and I checked out all the girls who entered through the rear door. Occasionally, depending on who we saw, we'd nudge each other and whisper comments like, "Hail Mary, look at that one!" or "Dear Lord!"

Each time the door opened, there was a split second of anticipation before we saw who it was. After a while, it got so that we could guess who it was based on the sound the door made.

When it was time for Holy Communion, we took a grand circle tour to the altar to check out the people on the other side. After a few moments of prayerful meditation back in our pew, we removed our hands from our faces and shared our insights and observations.

"Did you see that short chick with the pink hat near the holy water?"

"Hey, check out the one in the pew near St. Brigid!"

"What about the blonde chick up near St. Joseph?"

I thought to myself that if Sister D.P. were here, I'd be spending the rest of my life in hell, next to those radiators.

When Mass ended, the girls filed out, but we hung back to glance around one last time, blessing ourselves several times with holy water.

Lisa dutifully hurried ahead with Eileen, undoubtedly to brief her on our conversation, and Colleen subtly waited around for Pete. Then we all went back to the block to hang out for a while and make plans for the week ahead.

Chapter III

The BOMBERS

On weekdays our main activity was stickball, and the games began early, around ten in the morning. Sleeping late was one of the simple pleasures of summer vacation I enjoyed most, so I usually didn't arrive on the block until eleven thirty, near the end of the first game.

While most games were played between the guys from the block, we occasionally played teams from other blocks. Just about all the guys from the block were diehard Yankees fans, so in honor of the Bronx Bombers, our team was called the Woodbine Street BOMBERS. We even had team uniforms, which initially consisted of nothing more than jeans, sneakers, and white T-shirts with "BOMBERS" printed across the front with black Magic Marker. Later we upgraded the shirts with black iron-on letters purchased for two cents apiece up at Joe's Army and Navy store. On the back of our shirts were our numbers, usually the one held by our favorite ballplayer. For example, Pete had number seven for Mickey Mantle, Timmy had number twenty-eight for Joe Pepitone, Ralphie number one for Bobby Richardson, and I, the lone Dodgers fan on the team, number four for Duke Snider. Richie and M.C. both wanted nine, the number worn by Roger Maris of the Yankees. Maris hit sixty-one home runs the year before, breaking the old record of sixty, held by the legendary Babe Ruth. Maris's new record, however, came with controversy because it took him more games than Ruth to do it. Though the record was somewhat tainted by the asterisk that appeared next to it in the record books, Maris was still regarded by many kids as the modern-day home run hero. After a round of odds-and-evens, which M.C. won, Richie settled for number three, which had been worn by Ruth.

Our stickball court faced up the block toward Ridgewood Place and began at a sewer cover that served as home plate. First and third bases were initially outlined in chalk and eventually made more permanent with white paint that M.C. had snuck out of his grandfather's cellar. Second base was another sewer cover located seventy-five feet up the block. Any ball hit over the lumberyard fence, aka the chain-link monster, on a fly, was a home run. Those going over on a bounce were ground rule doubles. They happened on those rare occasions when we were using Pensy Pinky or Spaldeen high-bounce rubber balls, which cost the exorbitant price of thirty cents each. Fly balls hitting the buildings on either side of the street were fouls, as were those that bounced inside their gates before being caught. Pop flies landing on roofs were automatic outs unless by some act of luck they came back down, in which case they were only fouls. Grounders landing under parked cars in fair territory were all-you-could-get and made guys like little Ralphie key players on defense.

Broken windows usually resulted in a temporary delay of game, during which everyone ran like the hammers of hell. When the coast was clear, we gradually returned and resumed the game, acting as if nothing had happened.

One of the nice things about stickball was that it required a minimal amount of equipment: a few balls (at least one or two were lost every game); three or four gloves, depending on the number of players on each side; and one or two stickball bats.

The best gloves were the old worn-out kind that were ragged after years of abuse. Newer gloves were not as good because their hard pockets caused line drives to pop out. Old gloves were not only nice and soft but also convenient for throwing after grounders that might otherwise get jammed behind the wheels of parked cars and allow the hitter to take extra bases.

When it came to stickball bats, there were two basic models: those bought at Joe's Army and Navy store, specifically made for stickball, and those that had been broomsticks, specifically made for sweeping. The selection of bats often depended on whether a hitter was playing it safe and going for a base hit or risking the odds and trying for a home run. The store-bought bats had taped handles and were heavier and thicker. While they were a little more difficult to swing, they offered more surface area with which to make contact. The broomsticks, on the other hand, were much thinner, lighter, and longer, and made a whipping sound when swung. The odds of hitting with them were not as good, but when they did make contact, the ball took off like a rocket.

Players also used different techniques for hitting. Some tossed the ball up and let it bounce several times before swinging. Others would just toss the ball up and swing at it on the fly. Everyone stayed with the style that worked best for them until they got into a slump. Then the experimenting began.

When it came to choosing sides, teams mostly consisted of three players, sometimes four, depending on how many guys were around or the number of players on an opposing block's team. The Palmetto Royals from around the corner always insisted on four men. When we played them, our fourth man either backed up the outfielder near the lumberyard fence or played on the sidewalk if the batter was known to be a pull hitter.

Of all the positions on a team, the outfielder was perhaps the most important. In addition to playing the field, the outfielder was also responsible for keeping a lookout for approaching cars and then signaling to the rest of the players on the field. If the batter swung before the outfielder yelled *Car!* or *Time!*, the ball remained in play. Getting to it then became the problem of the fielding team, even if it meant dodging moving cars. If the batter swung after the signal, the swing didn't count, regardless of whether it was a strike or a home run.

That rule cost me the lone home run I hit that year. In a game against the Palmetto Royals, I was at the plate and a kid named Davey, their outfielder, called time as I was following through on my swing. The ball went sailing up and away, just clearing the top of the fence.

A home run!

I had finally done it!

Yes?

No!

"I called time before you swung!" Davey insisted. "The home run doesn't count!"

"Whaddaya mean it doesn't count!" I screamed as I banged my stick down on the ground, breaking the handle in the process.

"The ball went over the fence, and that's all there is to it,"

M.C. argued. "Next batter up."

Unfortunately, it wasn't that simple. The Royals were adamant about having called time before I swung, and after fifteen minutes of arguing, Pete tried to reach a compromise.

"Okay, okay, I have an idea," he suggested. "Since it's the first home run that Danny has hit, how about we let him count it on his record but not on the score?"

The proposal was acceptable to everyone except me.

"No way! No way!" I yelled. "If it doesn't count on the score, then I ain't counting it on my record."

If I was going to get a home run, I wanted it to be fair and square. I didn't want to be known as the Roger Maris of stickball!

Keeping that incident in mind whenever I played the outfield, I always struggled over whether to call time if a car was still some distance away. While I certainly wasn't crazy about dodging an oncoming car while chasing a fly ball, I also didn't want to stand around all day if some Sunday driver took their sweet time approaching and then passing the block.

After a while, I became familiar with the patterns of different drivers in the neighborhood based on the model cars they drove. One particularly annoying driver was a young guy who drove a black '62 Chevy Super Sport convertible that had red bucket seats and a loud 409 engine. He liked to cruise around the neighborhood and circle the block three or four times at a clip, his radio blasting and one arm dangling outside his car window. Each of his tours resulted in a delay of game as we hoped it would be his last trip. When we yelled at him to give us a break, it only made matters worse. He'd either come around the block again and go very slowly or, worse, he would return, roaring down the block and burning rubber while we all dodged out of his way.

After tolerating this for a while, we felt we needed to take matters into our own hands, so one day we bought small sharp tacks and waited for the creep to come around. When he arrived, we started yelling at him.

"C'mon, give us a break; we're trying to play a game!"

We hoped our protests would bring him around again, and sure enough they did.

When I spotted the creep approaching, I yelled, "Four-oh-nine!"—the signal to put our plan in place.

Upon hearing it, Pete and M.C. ran to the Irving Avenue corner and sprinkled a few boxes of the tacks near the stop sign where the creep usually peeled out. Then they raced back to home plate so that the creep wouldn't suspect anything when he turned onto the block.

As predicted, when the 409 turned onto the block, it crawled at a snail's pace. The creep had a smug look on his face as a cigarette sarcastically dangled from his lips. Meanwhile, we tried to change the tone of our voices from yells to pleas, hoping he would think we had given up, but more importantly, to divert his attention from the booby trap awaiting ahead.

When he reached the sign, he took an extra-long time, smiling at us in his rearview mirror, probably thinking he had won this latest round of his cruising challenge. Finally, he peeled out toward the next block, and when he got halfway down—BOOM!

The 409 screeched to a stop, and the creep leapt out of his car to check his front tires.

A blowout!

We all went wild, like young Davids who had just

conquered the mightier Goliath!

From that time on, the 409 creep didn't come around as often, and we took satisfaction in knowing that while we had not looked for trouble, we had found a way of dealing with it when it came our way.

Immediately after The Blowout Incident, things settled down. The guys got back to playing stickball while the girls got into the action as the "B Girls"—the official cheerleaders for the Bombers Stickball team—whenever we played other neighborhood teams.

The founding members of the B Girls were the Twins and Lisa. They wore white T-shirts with black Bs (from Joe's Army and Navy) ironed on the front. With trusty transistor radios in hand, the B Girls would stand near home plate and cheer us Bombers on when we were at bat and then heckle the other teams when it was their turn to hit. The B Girls also performed song-and-dance routines between innings and during the seventh-inning stretch!

Day in and day out, the routine was pretty much the same. Countless numbers of stickball games, the B Girls, lost balls, broken bats, and hoarse voices from yelling *Time!* and disputing close plays. After several hours of these activities each day, one might think we'd be too tired to do anything afterward.

Not so!

When the last stickball game ended, the crowd all went home to eat, get cleaned up, and return to the block as soon as possible in the early evening, when "other games" were played.

Chapter IV

"Other Games"

Although my route along Irving Avenue was the same, the walk home from Woodbine Street often felt empty and seemed to take longer than the trek there. In many ways, it was like a journey between two separate worlds. On the block, I felt like I belonged, had some control over my life, and could relate to everyone on an equal basis. In my other world, I behaved the way I was expected to by my teachers, parents, and family members. As a result, the trip between my house and the block often brought a rise or fall of my spirits, depending on the direction I was heading.

When I finally reached my house, I would open the outer front door into the hallway vestibule and then hop up one flight of stairs, two steps at a time, to the front door of the four-room railroad apartment I shared with my mother, father, and older brother. Our building contained three other similar apartments and two stores on the ground floor. One store was a vacant knitting mill; unfortunately, the other one was a sheet-metal shop, where Harry, the owner, banged away at all hours of the day and night making racks for grocery stores and bakeries. Between Harry and the Myrtle Avenue El that frequently rattled past our house, there were very few quiet moments. However, after a few years of living there, we got used to all the noises and hardly noticed them.

Whenever I entered our apartment, my mother's greeting was always the same: "Hi honey, how was your day? Anything new?"

Most of the time I'd keep my responses short, like "Uh, okay" or "Nothing much," in the hopes that my answer would not generate more questions. On those rare occasions when we actually talked, I'd hear maternal advice about how things weren't quite as serious as I was taking them or, worse, I'd get teased by my brother about whatever new girl I liked. These were the last things I wanted to hear because as far as I and the others on the block were concerned, everything that happened on Woodbine Street was important and needed to be taken very seriously!

As soon as I finished supper, I'd quickly get ready to head back to the block. I'd wash up and exchange my black-lettered Fruit of the Loom Bomber T-shirt for a fresh, colored one to spruce up a little. Then I'd spend time at the bathroom mirror combing and recombing my hair until it was just right. When I got the swirl in front exactly the way I liked it, I'd take one last look, kiss my mother goodbye, and try to give my brother a surprise punch in the arm before barreling out the apartment door. (My father worked nights as a trailer driver at the Brooklyn Navy Yard, and I didn't see him much except on weekends.) Upon closing the apartment door and entering the hallway, I'd hop onto the stairway banister and slide down, landing inches from the front door. Outside, the warm breeze of early evening often combined with the glow of a soon-to-be-setting sun, quickly recharged me for the games we would soon be playing .

The journey back to the block was now measured by

familiar markings along the way. The first block had a calendar factory on it that always displayed the current month's pinup on its front door. On the next block stood an auto supply store with the latest racing equipment showcased in its front window. Then came a block with a big billboard illustrating life-sized advertisements of the latest-model cars. At Gates Avenue, the halfway point, I'd sprint across to dodge oncoming buses that approached from either direction. Just beyond Gates Avenue came a block of small, shingled one-family houses, then a block with a German delicatessen, whose front entrance had two gumball machines chained down to an oil delivery pipe. When I finally reached the Washington Irving branch of the public library, I'd scoot across Irving Avenue and head toward the corner that turned onto the block.

I loved the feeling I had whenever I reached that corner, like a performer going onstage just before the curtain rose. With a surge of adrenaline, I'd turn the corner and quickly scan the block to see if anyone was in sight. If no one was out, I'd head directly for Timmy's or Pete's house to ring their bell and let them know I had arrived. Sometimes I just waited on their stoop, content to know that I was back where the action would soon start. On other occasions, I might be invited in.

At Timmy's, I was always offered an eight-ounce bottle of Coke while I waited for him and stayed clear of his dog, Scotty, who had a bad habit of growling and snapping at strangers.

Over at Pete's house, I would be directed by his father, Steve, to sit down and join the family for lasagna or spaghetti while he kidded me about never refusing a free meal.

On those rare times when someone might already be out on

the block by the time I arrived, we'd sit on a stoop, replay that day's events, and make plans for the evening ahead. Over a short period of time, other members of the crowd would come charging out of their houses one by one, like football players eager to resume the second half of a game. Since Pete had the largest family, he usually took the longest to eat dinner, and once he arrived, plans for the evening were quickly put into action.

In contrast to the games we played during the day, the ones we played at night were completely co-ed in nature, with the girls participating equally with the guys. Sometimes we played ring-a-lievio, a game like tag but with two teams: the Chasers and the Chasees. The object of the game was for the Chasers to capture all the Chasees. Capturing someone involved chasing and holding them while yelling, "Ring a lievio one-two-three, one-two-three, one-two-three!" Once someone was captured, they had to stay in an area called the den, which was closely guarded. There they would remain captive until their teammates were either captured or freed by a team member who successfully broke into the den and yelled, "Free all!"

During ring-a-lievio, selection of the teams involved getting the right combination of speed and strength. Pete and I were the two fastest on the block, so we usually chose for sides. When it came to strength, one of the most sought-after players was Lisa. When she guarded the den, no one, but no one, got past her, and there were many who literally lost their shirts trying.

When we didn't play ring-a-lievio, we played another game specially created by the crowd. Best described as a combination of ring-a-lievio and post office, this game was known and loved by all as Payoff.

Payoff also involved two teams, except one consisted of all girls and the other all guys. Each team had a captain who represented their side during the opening coin toss, the outcome of which determined who did the chasing. The object of the game was to catch a member of the opposing team and yell, "Payoff!" Once that happened, the guy and the girl went for the payoff, which involved making out in a cellar doorway underneath one of the stoops.

The first time I played Payoff, I felt extremely nervous. While I had kissed girls on the lips a few times during games of spin the bottle, the idea of doing it continuously over a prolonged period was mind-boggling. Later, when I got the hang of it, I found the experience to be like swimming. Once you got the breathing down, you could do it forever. When it came to making out, everyone had their own style. Some just kissed on the lips, while others liked the more advanced technique of "tongue kissing." This latter approach, however, required special skill and could get a little sloppy if you didn't know what you were doing. Most of the time when people made out, they kept their eyes closed but might occasionally open one or both to peek. I found that whenever I opened an eye to peek, the girl I was with always seemed to choose that same moment to look, and we'd both end up laughing. Making out and peeking was okay; staring, however, was definitely "played out," a term we frequently used to mean "not cool."

I quickly discovered that playing Payoff wasn't as simple as I thought it would be. Initially, I figured it would give me a chance to make out with Eileen and perhaps even get her to like me. Catching her, however, was not that easy because she stayed close to Pete and wasn't about to let me sidetrack her. Colleen also tried to get caught by Pete and made no secret of it. So while Pete found himself in the enviable position of having the choice of Eileen or Colleen, I felt like I had the plague. To further complicate matters, we let Nancy and Linda, two younger girls, play along so that we could get equal sides. Unfortunately, they often screwed things up by placing themselves in the middle of the action in hopes of getting caught.

The first night I played Payoff, I finally caught Eileen, but only after Colleen got herself caught by Pete. Unfortunately, when we got to a cellar doorway to make out, Eileen's sad expression took all the fun out of it for me. I kissed her once, and while she dutifully obliged, I could tell her heart wasn't in it. I asked her if she wanted to stop, and she nodded. After we walked back up the steps, she sprinted to her house. I scanned the block and, seeing no surface activity, headed home.

When I arrived at my house, my mother asked me why I was home so early. I told her that there weren't many kids out that night, which in an odd way was the truth since most of them were down in cellar doorways making out.

I took a cold shower and then headed to bed. Once I settled in, I repeatedly replayed the scene with Eileen in the cellar doorway, hoping for a different outcome. In a short while, I realized I had a lot to learn about girls and felt like I had just gotten my first lesson.

Perhaps letting a girl know right away that I liked her was not the best way to play it. Perhaps more planning was required, along with a strategy to get whomever I liked to like me first. Once that happened, then maybe I could let them know I liked them.

Yeah, that was probably it. That was the way to play it. I was finally getting the idea!

Having completed my first lesson, I fluffed up my pillow and drifted off to sleep, ready and eager to apply what I had learned in the many days ahead.

Chapter V

The Thrill of Victory and the Agony of Defeat

The days and weeks of summer slipped by quickly, and before we knew it, it was already the middle of August. Robert Hall back-to-school clothing commercials were the first dreaded sign that our remaining days of vacation were winding down to a precious few.

Except for Timmy, Ralphie, and me, everyone on the Bombers stickball team had hit a home run over the lumberyard fence. A husky German kid named George, who lived up on Ridgewood Place and only showed up on the block for stickball games, was the home run leader. Pete was second, M.C. third, and Richie fourth. As the stickball season approached its conclusion, the crowd's attention shifted from who had hit the most home runs to who might hit his first. Since Ralphie was mainly a singles and doubles hitter, the real race for the fence boiled down to Timmy and me. Although we both had come close on a few occasions, each of us was still looking for our first home run with every at bat. With time running out, the pressure and drama mounted, but the harder we tried to reach the fence, the farther away it seemed.

On paper, Timmy had a slight edge. He was physically bigger than I was and over a year older. As a lefty hitter, he also had a better chance of pulling the ball over several short garages on the northeast corner of the block. In contrast, as a righty, I needed to hit the ball straight to avoid tall six-family houses that lined the northwest corner. In addition, in the area where I was likely to reach the lumberyard, a portion of its two-story administration building jutted out. Although the home run mark on the building was the same height as the fence, the taller building made it appear more difficult.

During the remainder of the stickball season, excitement on the block mounted with each game. It was our version of the great home run race from the year before, when Mickey Mantle and Roger Maris competed to break Babe Ruth's record.

I felt mounting pressure and frustration whenever I was at bat, and after, putting everything I had into a swing, only to see my hit fade into the outfielder's glove. The harder I swung, the shorter the ball seemed to go, especially after a rare occasion when I reached the sidewalk in front of the lumberyard fence.

On days when Timmy and I weren't coming close to the fence, we would take a break from playing and go for a walk on Myrtle Avenue, where we'd check out footballs and other winter sports equipment already on display in the front window of Joe's Army and Navy store. On the trip back, we'd sometimes take a detour along Wycoff Avenue to Joan's Pet Shop. There, in addition to looking at the usual assortment of dogs, cats, and parakeets, we'd spend time peering into tall glass tanks, where Joan kept a large selection of tropical lizards.

"Hey, check out the midget dinosaurs!" M.C. exclaimed. "They look like the ones in the *Godzilla* movies!"

Timmy had an interest in zoology and quickly corrected M.C. "No way, dummy! That's an iguana. Don't you know anything?"

"I knew that!" M.C. said. "I was only kidding."

Oddly, when Timmy had spoken, the iguana glanced at him with a look of satisfaction, as though pleased that someone had finally gotten its name correct.

After more small talk, we asked Joan how much the iguana cost.

"Seven dollars and fifty cents, plus tax."

Seven-fifty? She might as well have said seven hundred and fifty!

Still, it seemed like Timmy really liked that ugly thing that kept staring at him with its camera-shutter eyes and long thin tongue snapping in and out like a retractable tape measure.

On the way back from the pet store, we kept talking about the iguana. Then Pete came up with what he thought was a bright idea. "Hey, whaddaya say if Timmy hits it over the fence, we all chip in and get him the iguana?"

Great. I needed Timmy to have another incentive like I needed a hole in the head. However, we all agreed, both to encourage him and to add more excitement to the race for the fence.

A few days later, we were playing our usual number of games, and because the season was almost over, we decided to use Pensy Pinkies and Spaldeens to liven things up a bit. Both Timmy and I had abandoned the safety of the Joe's Army and Navy bats for the long-ball broomsticks. When either of us was at bat, there would be chants of encouragement from the

B Girls: "C'mon, Danny, smack that ball!" or "Okay, Timmy, let's do it!"

The shots I hit were all high and initially looked like they might have the range. Some landed as far as the sidewalk in front of the lumberyard, while others fell far short. Timmy's shots, on the other hand, were line drives that started out low and then rose like golf balls driven off a tee. On a few occasions, he hit the lumberyard fence but just missed clearing it.

With each at bat, the tension mounted. We all sensed it was just a matter of time before one of us made it.

Then, finally, one of us did!

Timmy and I were both on the same team. He was at home plate, and I was sitting nearby on the bumper of a parked car. I kept my eyes glued on him as he tossed up the ball, let it bounce once, then twice, then swung and missed. SWOOSH, strike one!

Again, he tossed the ball up, one bounce, two bounces, then barely tipped it. Strike two!

Finally, on his next swing, he tossed up the ball, let it bounce and, without taking his eyes off it, whipped the broomstick around with all his might.

The stick contacted the ball with a stinging sound, and it took off like a rocket. Timmy dropped the stick and watched the flight of the ball as it sailed upward and veered slightly to the right. After what seemed liked the longest two seconds ever recorded, the ball bounced victoriously onto a pile of lumber located on the other side of the fence. When it hit the wood, cheers went up from everyone.

"It's over!"

"He did it!"

"Timmy hit it over!"

"Way to go, Timmy!"

In a gesture of triumph and relief, Timmy threw up his hands and cried, "It's about time!"

Then he took a victory trot around the bases, and all the fielders slapped him five as he passed them. He had just experienced the sweet thrill of victory and looked like he was floating on air.

Meanwhile, back on the car bumper, I found myself suffering the agony of defeat. When I saw Timmy's ball clear the fence, my heart sank down into my P.F. Flyers.

Those in my immediate vicinity sensed how I felt. Pete and the B Girls quickly glanced over in my direction as Timmy rounded the bases. In that brief moment, the empathetic looks in their eyes conveyed to me that they knew how I felt, and my disappointment began to dissolve. By the time Timmy reached home plate and jumped on it with both feet, I was there to greet him.

"Congratulations, Timmy!" I said in the strongest voice I could muster.

"Thanks a lot, D. I'm sorry it couldn't have been both of us."

Thanks to M.C.'s sense of humor, the awkwardness of the moment was short-lived.

"Hey, Timmy!" he shouted, running in from the outfield. "I can't wait to see the look on your mother's face when you walk into your house with that midget dinosaur!"

We all cracked up and then headed to the German delicatessen for celebratory sodas.

We returned with Pepsis and spent the remainder of the day reliving Timmy's moment of glory and discussing how we'd spend the remaining days of our vacation. For all practical purposes, Timmy's home run had marked the official end of the 1962 season of the Woodbine Street BOMBERS.

Chapter VI

A Winning Season

Following Timmy's home run, our remaining days of summer were spent preparing for a big party in celebration of the Bombers' winning season. The team's record had been thirteen wins and no losses, with just about all the wins coming at the expense of the Palmetto Royals.

Our plans called for the party to be held down in Timmy's cellar. Mamie, the landlady of Timmy's house, loved him like a grandson and was more than willing to let us use her cellar, providing we cleaned it before and after the party. Timmy, Pete, M.C., some of the others, and I spent several days down there, tying up bundles of yellowed newspapers and carting off old birdcages and fish tanks that had accumulated over the years. We also whitewashed the walls and made futile attempts to sweep the concrete floor, doing little more than pushing dust around from one end of the room to the other.

Throughout the cleanup project, the Twins and Lisa faithfully provided moral support by sitting outside near one of the small, screened cellar windows. With a trusty transistor radio in hand, they provided words of encouragement, telling us how well the cellar was coming along while switching radio stations back and forth between Murray the "K" on WINS and Cousin Brucie on WABC.

At the time, the most frequently played songs were "The Loco-Motion" by Little Eva and "Beechwood 4-5789" by The Marvelettes. The girls were also particularly excited about the latest Pick Hit of the Week, a song called "Sherry" by a new group called The Four Seasons. When it got played, they would call out to us, and we'd all stop what we were doing to listen and judge for ourselves. Even though it was newly released, the girls already knew the words and sang right along.

That summer, the popular dances were the Twist, the Locomotion, and the Mashed Potato, all of which had been introduced by songs with similar names. Just about all the dances involved little or no contact between partners, and in a change from the past, when kids imitated adults, it felt like older people were copying us. In terms of difficulty, the Twist was the easiest to learn, and everyone did it. The Locomotion, on the other hand, was more difficult and performed primarily by the girls. The most complicated of the dances was the Mashed Potato, which had been introduced by Dee Dee Sharp in a record called "It's Mashed Potato Time" and then again in a follow-up record with the catchy title "Gravy (For My Mashed Potatoes)." Pete could do it well, and while we were cleaning, he tried in vain to teach me. "Just pretend you're squashing out a bug with one foot while lifting up the other, then alternate."

Mashing out an imaginary bug with one foot was easy. Trying to move both feet simultaneously, however, was another story, and I often stumbled when I tried. Since everyone could do the twist and only the girls did the Locomotion, I figured that if I could learn the Mashed Potato, I might have a good chance of dancing with the girl of my choice. To speed up learning the moves, I bought a copy of "Gravy" and played it over and over while practicing in front of my bedroom mirror. For hours, I practiced mashing out a bug with one foot while simultaneously picking up the other one, then alternating. Over and over.

The catchy lyrics—with endless requests for gravy—could be heard blasting from my room nonstop.

After countless hours of practice, I was losing hope, but the day before the party, a switch in my head suddenly turned on. As if by reflex, I could move my feet simultaneously. I could hardly believe it. I danced for another hour just to make sure I wouldn't forget, then I rushed off to the block, stopping along the way to check that I hadn't lost it. At Gates Avenue, I got strange looks from several bus passengers when I crossed the street doing the Mashed Potato.

Upon finally arriving on the block, I Mashed Potatoed my way over to Pete's house to show him. We slapped each other five, then he proceeded to show me some fancier steps that not even the girls knew.

When the party began, I'd be ready to dance up a storm!

In addition to my success with the Mashed Potato, our collective efforts in the basement had produced impressive results. In a matter of a few days, the once-cluttered, dusty cellar had undergone a marvelous transformation. We'd draped red, yellow, and green strips of crepe paper from water pipes that ran along the ceiling, and we'd taped balloons on all the walls. Several handmade posters were also posted on the walls, some highlighting the Bombers' victories and others reminding people not to throw cups or paper plates on the floor.

A key task before the party had been the all-important one

of selecting which records to play. Each of us had contributed whatever we had to a common pool from which the final selections were made. The owners had carefully labeled their names on each record to ensure their safe return. I'd felt a little awkward because the only records I owned were a Fats Domino album and a record by Stan Freiberg called "The Yellow Rose of Texas," which previously belonged to my brother.

Thanks to the Twins and Lisa, who usually bought records as soon as they came out, we had a wide selection of the latest music to choose from. The 45s sold for sixty-five cents apiece, with occasional specials of two for a dollar or one free with every five purchased. Most of the time, the girls bought different records and then swapped them. Sometimes, however, there was a record they each desperately had to have, such as "Beechwood 4-5789" and "Sherry."

After the initial collection had been narrowed down to a select thirty, the next major step had been determining the order in which they would be played. Faster songs would usually be played early in the evening and slower ones later, after things had warmed up a bit. We all planned to take turns operating the record player and, depending on who was in charge, a record might get selected out of order if it was a favorite of that person or intended to communicate a "special message." As it happened, when Eileen was at the controls that night, she played a song by Neil Sedaka—"Breaking Up Is Hard To Do"—for Pete's benefit. Timmy's favorite was "409," the flip side of "Surfin' Safari" by the Beach Boys. When my turn came, I made sure that "Gravy" got played, and I even managed to sneak in about thirty seconds of "The Yellow Rose of Texas" before the others threatened it with destruction. Other songs like "Sherry" and "Beechwood 4-5789" must have been played a dozen times each.

Prior to the party, there'd been a hot rumor flying around that Pete might ask Lisa for a slow dance. This had been interpreted as a possible sign of more serious things to come. Eileen, Colleen, and Lisa had all made no secret that they liked Pete. Since he had already gone out with Eileen and had made out with Colleen during Payoff, it seemed only logical that Lisa was next in line—a notion she did little to discourage. A major issue for Lisa was whether to put her head on Pete's shoulders and/or to hold him around his neck or waist if they did dance. Another issue was whether Pete would do a one-step slow dance or a two-step *sloooowwer* dance. To be on the safe side, Lisa practiced both ways. The rest of us were very curious about how Eileen would react. Although it had been a while since she and Pete had broken up, she made it clear that she still regarded him as her exclusive territory, with a hands-off warning to any girls who might think otherwise.

Pete and I had held several conversations about his dance plans while cleaning the cellar. Though he acknowledged to me his plan to dance with Lisa, I still sensed he might get back together with Eileen after seeing her at the party—because the girls were reputedly pulling out all the stops. Rumor had it that they were buying new dresses and even getting permanents! When I told him that I thought he would wind up back with Eileen, he'd denied it so vehemently that we almost got into a fight over it.

Finally, the big night arrived. The party began at seven, and my mother had agreed to let me stay out until ten on the condition that she came and met me. While this embarrassed me to no end, my desire to stay out longer was a strong incentive for me to go along with her condition.

In preparation for the party, I dry-cleaned my best and only suit. As I checked myself out in the bathroom mirror, I felt pretty cool in my tailored suit, skintight pegged pants, white tab shirt, thin V-knotted tie, pearl tiepin, and black pointy shoes with matching Ban-Lon socks. After one last look in the mirror, I strutted out of the house feeling like a million dollars.

When I arrived, just about everyone was there, including Timmy's mother. To our disappointment she insisted on staying around just to make sure we "behaved."

Everyone was dressed to the nines, and the girls looked great with their permanents. At first, everyone just sat around, girls on one side and guys on the other. Then the girls got up and danced when "The Loco-Motion" came on. When "Mashed Potato Time" came on, Pete and I got up and danced with Eileen and Colleen. Initially I was a little wobbly, but I quickly loosened up and tried some fancier crossover steps. When "The Twist" came on, everyone, including little Ralphie, stood up and danced. From that moment on, the ice was broken, and the party became a huge success. Before the night was over, Pete did that slow dance with Lisa, but as I predicted, he later wound up asking Eileen out again.

Near the party's end, all the members of the 1962 Woodbine Street Bombers Stickball Team gathered around to have our picture taken, just as the major league teams did at the end of their season. We held a sign that M.C. had made expressly for the occasion. It listed the names of the team members along with statistics on their batting averages, home runs, and runs batted in. Next to my name, a "1" was listed under home runs, with "(Hit during time-out)" written underneath.

At the top, the poster read: "CONGRATULATIONS 1962 BOMBERS ON A WINNING SEASON!"

When I looked around, it felt like light-years had passed since that eventful first day when I arrived on the block.

As far as I was concerned, that sign said it all. That summer had truly been a winning season.

One I would never forget.

Chapter VII

CLEAN LIVING

A few weeks after the Bomber Party, we were all back to school, and life on the block slowed down a bit. Pete was in his second year at Thomas Edison Vocational High; the Twins, M.C., and Lisa were all in the eighth grade at St. Brigid's; and Timmy and I were in our last year at Halsey Junior High.

In mid-October, the Cuban Missile Crisis occurred. As the world held its breath in fear of World War III, the big news on the block was a weightlifting exhibition M.C.'s father had planned for all the guys to demonstrate the benefits of CLEAN LIVING.

From the looks of him, Mr. C, M.C.'s father, did not have the appearance of a weightlifter. He was a short, nervous man in his early forties, who wore glasses, worked at the local supermarket, and looked like he worked at the local supermarket. In contrast to M.C.'s grandfather, the younger Mr. C had a mild demeanor, a trait frequently abused by M.C. and his younger brothers, Gerald and Clark, particularly when Mr. C called them up for dinner. The dinner-call routine was always the same. After several rounds of calls and blatant nonresponses, Mr. C, in a voice cracking with rage, would resort to threatening his sons with The Strap. Sometimes he went as far as actually chasing them around the street!

On the night of the weightlifting exhibition, we arrived at M.C.'s house at seven o'clock sharp. He and his family lived in an apartment in the three-family house owned by his grandfather. After we settled into their small living room, Mrs. C, who in many ways was a female version of Mr. C, offered us soda, milk, and cookies. After we ate our fill, the exhibition began.

"CLEAN LIVING," Mr. C said in a loud and emphatic voice. "You've got to treat your bodies as though they are finely tuned machines that will develop terrible problems if you don't take care of them!"

We all stared at him and waited to hear what was next.

"Do you know what will cause those problems, boys?"

"Bad gas?" Timmy cracked.

We all snickered and poked each other. All of us, that is, except for M.C., who didn't appreciate our humor. Mr. C smiled briefly, looking like he'd forgotten what he planned to say. Then he remembered and continued.

"Alcohol and tobacco, boys," he blurted out. "ALCOHOL AND TOBACCO!"

After fifteen more minutes or so of the clean-living lecture, we were ready to throw up. It began to feel like a revival meeting. Every time Mr. C mentioned clean living, we all responded, "That's right, nooo smoking and nooo drinking!" in the hopes that he'd believe we'd gotten the message and would move on to the main event.

Finally, the moment we had all been waiting for arrived. Mr. C took off his shirt, and the mild-mannered grocery clerk revealed that he was really a muscular Man of Steel.

Halfway through the exhibition, our attention turned away

from Mr. C and onto M.C.'s four-year-old brother, Clark, who began to shinny up one of the yet-unneeded heating pipes that ran from floor to ceiling. Clark made it three-quarters of the way up the pipe, then prepared to leap onto a nearby china cabinet. It was quite a scene.

Unaware of Clark's pending feat, Mr. C turned beet red as he lifted barbells while espousing the merits of clean living. But we were all nudging each other and quietly rooting for Clark to jump onto the cabinet. When Mr. C finally caught on, he dropped the weights to the floor with a thundering sound and screamed at Clark, who was peering down from the top of the cabinet like King Kong on top of the Empire State Building.

A short while later, the exhibition ended, and we filed out of M.C.'s house, thanking Mrs. C for the food and vowing to Mr. C that we'd lead CLEAN LIVES from that day forward. Then we congratulated the real hero of the night, little Clark, for reaching new heights in his climbing pursuits.

Soon after the exhibition, M.C. and Pete began lifting weights together at M.C.'s house, and Timmy and I decided that we would start lifting in Timmy's cellar. Two or three nights a week after school, I'd go over to Timmy's for an hour to lift, do sit-ups, and listen to records. We used an old cellar storage room that had been renovated into a clubroom several years earlier by Timmy's older brother. The room contained all the essentials of adolescent life: an old dresser with a mirror to watch ourselves as we worked out; convenient drawers for storing soda; a bulletin board for posting pictures of Dan Lurie and other bodybuilding idols; a table with a record player on it; a stack of the latest 45s; and, last but not least, a set of barbells. We made a workout bench by nailing together wooden milk boxes, and we used an old mat for sit-ups.

We developed exercise routines based on weightlifting magazines we had found and followed them religiously. After a couple of months, Timmy and I developed some rather decent builds. We also became good friends and sometimes listened to records and shot the bull about current events on the block.

Every so often when we were working out, Timmy's father would come downstairs, open a locked storage bin in the front of the cellar, turn on a pull-chain light, and go in, closing the door behind him. An hour later he would reappear, lock the door, and return upstairs. This happened at least once a week, and out of curiosity, I asked Timmy what his father did in there.

"Oh, that's my father's library," he said with a chuckle. "He goes in there to catch up on his reading."

His laughter hinted that there was more to it, but I decided not to pursue the issue. Still, whenever I passed the door to his father's bin, I wondered what was really on the other side.

Library? Reading? What could Timmy have meant?

It seemed to me that if Timmy's father wanted to read, he could just as easily have done it upstairs in the comfort of his apartment. If it was a matter of needing peace and quiet, why didn't he go to the library around the corner? Why use a cellar bin, particularly in the winter, that was so cold and damp?

One night after we finished working out and Timmy's father had come and gone, Timmy took a key out of his pocket and showed it to me.

"Guess what this is?" he asked in a mischievous voice.

"A key," I responded matter-of-factly. "So what? Are we

51

going to play treasure hunt with it?"

"Ha so!" he replied, his voice taking on the tone of Charlie Chan, the famous Chinese detective. "In a manner of speaking, we *are* going to play treasure hunt. The key you see before you is no *ordinary* key. This little baby opens the door to my father's library!"

The key to the mysterious room!!!

There it was!

I looked at it again, only this time with a newfound reverence.

Then, moving with the precision of a top-secret commando operation, we proceeded with our assault on the bin.

"You keep a lookout while I head for the door," Timmy commanded. "If it looks like someone's coming, cough loudly."

He headed out while I listened for hostile sounds.

When he reached the bin, he quickly opened the door and waved me in. "C'mon, c'mon, hurry up!"

I sprinted toward the door. As soon as I arrived, Timmy pulled me in, closed the door, then yanked a chain to turn on the bare bulb fixture dangling from the ceiling.

Once the light came on, I couldn't believe my eyes!

There before us lay hundreds of adult magazines in all their graphic splendor. Additionally, there were several decks of French cards and assorted novelty items. One item especially caught my eye: a transparent ballpoint pen in which a bikini-clad girl dropped when the pen was turned down to write. Compared to a sneaked thirty-second glance through *Playboy* at the local newsstand, this room was the answer to an adolescent boy's dreams—a mother lode of sex education!

For safety's sake, we quickly picked out three intriguing

magazines from the middle of a pile, being careful not to disturb those on top in case they had been organized in a secretly coded manner. Then we scurried back to the clubroom to inspect our bounty in all its glorious detail. At first it felt a little strange having so much time to look at the pictures without some voice yelling at us from behind a newsstand counter. Slowly we turned the pages, examining them repeatedly and leaving no detail overlooked. First the face, then the breasts, then the rear end, and then more private areas (if we had truly lucked out on a good magazine), and then back to the face to begin the process all over again. Whenever I looked at the pictures, I always found myself thinking that somewhere this woman might be walking around fully clothed, and now I, in the sanctity of this little room, was seeing her as few men had (probably no more than a few thousand, anyway).

If a magazine was very good, we'd hide it safely away in a hole in the drop ceiling, where large, insulated water pipes ran through the room. Sometimes Timmy's mother would come clanking down the old wooden steps near the front of the cellar, followed by her familiar call of, "Tim-meeeeeeee!"

Then we'd fold the magazines in half and shove them into the hole.

On one occasion Timmy's mother didn't call his name, and we were so engrossed in the material that we didn't hear her coming until she was just outside the door of the workout room. We scurried around in muffled shock and fear, trying to jam the magazines into the hole and caring little about whether we could retrieve them again. When we opened the door, we tried to act calm, but Timmy's mother asked us why it had been so quiet when she first came down.

Luckily, we kept our cool and deftly handled the cross-examination.

"Hello, Mrs. M, how are you?" I said, trying to keep her facing toward me and away from the hole in the ceiling.

"Why did you boys have this door locked, and what was all that commotion in there?" she shot back suspiciously.

"We kept the door locked because it was damp outside," Timmy said. "We were sweating and didn't want to catch a cold."

Yeah, that was it! The old health angle! What mother could argue with a son who was trying not to catch a cold? *Way to go, Timmy!*

"Well, why did I hear so much noise in there once I approached?"

"We were moving some weights around," I responded in my best Eddie Haskell *Leave It To Beaver* voice. "We were laughing about how it was harder to move the weights around than to lift them."

Meanwhile, I was praying to the magazine in the ceiling: *C'mon, you breasts, hold up a little longer.* Because if that magazine fell through, we were dead meat!

"Well, okay," she replied, her voice returning to normal range. "But be quiet! It's late!"

"Anything you say, Mom."

We were almost home free.

No sooner had Timmy's mother closed the door behind her and clanked back up the stairs than the magazine dropped to the floor with a plopping sound, revealing the centerfold in flagrante! Timmy and I stared at the magazine and then at each other. Realizing the implications had it fallen moments sooner, we fell to the floor rolling in muffled laughter, vowing to each other to live CLEAN LIVES and, more importantly, to find alternate hiding places for our reading materials in the event of similar close calls in the future!

Chapter VIII

Close Encounters

During the weekends, we took a break from weightlifting and played touch football in the street. If the entire crowd was around, we congregated up the block in the doorway of the old knitting mill, where we tried to hit harmony to our favorite songs. The guys, most of whose voices were changing, found it somewhat of a struggle to sing falsetto like the Four Seasons in "Sherry" and their latest hit, "Big Girls Don't Cry."

After making up with Eileen at the Bomber party, Pete was out of circulation, so Colleen and Lisa focused their attention on Timmy. One night after the guys finished singing, Colleen and Lisa pretended to be a popular female group called the Crystals and could be heard singing Timmy's favorite song, "He's A Rebel."

When we weren't hitting harmony, we got into animated conversations about any number of topics to keep our minds off the cold weather. One of the more frequent topics was the "race for space" between the United States and Russia to land a man on the moon first. During the prior two years, there were daily reports in newspapers about American and Russian manned space launchings. The American Mercury astronauts—Shepherd, Grissom, Glenn, Carpenter, Schirra, and Cooper—had practically become household names. Each of their successive flights was longer and more complex than the previous one and included important experiments to help meet President Kennedy's challenge of landing an American on the moon before the end of the decade.

On the block, the possibility of flying in space also captured our imaginations. Based on pictures we had seen on television, we speculated about what it must feel like to float around weightlessly.

"Imagine playing stickball on the moon!" I said.

"Yeah, wouldn't that be boss?" Pete responded.

"Could you imagine floating up in the air to catch a fly ball?" M.C. said. "No one would ever be able to hit a home run."

"I know how that feels," I responded kiddingly.

"How about all of those balls that wind up on the roofs?" Timmy added. "We'd be able to float up and get them. A Spalding would last an entire summer!"

One Saturday when M.C. and Pete weren't around, Timmy and I discussed outer space in the clubroom, which resulted in our launching a silly adolescent prank on our unsuspecting friends.

"There's gotta be somebody out there among all those galaxies," I insisted as I sipped hot chocolate we'd made to keep warm.

"Oh yeah, definitely!" Timmy agreed. "Sooner or later, either we're going to find them or they're going to find us."

"Wouldn't it be wild if people from other planets were already here?" I said, my imagination getting the best of me.

"Yeah, like in one of those episodes of *The Twilight Zone*."

Just then, Timmy's dog, Scotty, appeared, signaling with a bark that it was time for his walk.

Our conversation continued as Timmy fixed a leash to Scotty's collar.

"What if beings from outer space were already here in the form of animals?" he suggested. "For all we know, Scotty might be one of them. After all, I did find him abandoned as a puppy!"

I looked at Scotty and he looked at me. His tongue was hanging out and his tail was wagging at a steady beat.

"Yeah, what if his real name was ZoZo or something like that?"

At the sound of the name ZoZo, Scotty's ears perked up, and Timmy and I both laughed.

"Hey," Timmy exclaimed, "we oughta tell Pete and M.C. that Scotty spoke to us and told us he's from another planet!"

"Wouldn't that be wild! But we gotta make it believable."

During Scotty's walk, we worked out the details of our mischievous plan.

When we returned, I headed down to the room while Timmy stopped in at his apartment. A few minutes later he returned, lugging a large tape recorder we planned to use to record our conversations with the alien being, ZoZo.

We started the tape with some excerpts from "Telstar," a popular song written to commemorate the first American communications satellite. Following the brief musical introduction, Timmy slowly produced the deep voice of the mysterious ZoZo.

"My name is ZoZo," he said robotically. "I am a visitor from the planet Zo, which is located in a far-off galaxy. I have come to your planet Earth in the form of a dog in order to better study human beings."

"Why did you come to Woodbine Street?" I asked, being

sure to talk into the microphone.

"My spacecraft landed near some processed wood not far from this location."

"Hey, that must be the lumberyard," I said to Timmy, trying to sound startled.

"That's right!" Timmy responded in his regular voice. "I still can't believe this!"

"Me neither," I said.

"I have come to earth with special powers," ZoZo said.

"Like what?" I asked, playing the straight man.

"I can fly, walk up walls, and hang suspended from ceilings."

"How about showing us?" Timmy asked.

We pretended to see ZoZo flying, walking up walls, and hanging from the ceiling.

"Hey, better duck, Timmy!" I screamed. "He's flying pretty low! I don't believe what I'm seeing."

"Me neither, D. He's actually walking along the ceiling. Lookathat!"

"As you have just witnessed," ZoZo said, "I can perform a number of feats which are beyond those of humans."

"What else can you do?" I asked, suppressing my giggling.

"I can also move heavy objects with my mind."

Timmy picked up a small weight and, with the microphone close by, dropped it on the concrete floor to simulate the sound of a heavy object being thrown across the room.

"As you have just witnessed," ZoZo continued, "I can move the weight merely by thinking about it."

"Amazing!" I said.

"I still don't believe what I'm seeing!" Timmy added for effect.

Then we turned off the tape recorder and planned the next steps. Timmy went upstairs, got Scotty, and took him to the backyard, where Scotty ran around in the dirt. After a few minutes, Timmy picked him up and held him like a baby, being careful not to get any dirt on himself from Scotty's paws.

Once back in the clubroom, Timmy headed to the dresser and let Scotty stand on top, just as ZoZo had done when he "landed" there after flying around the room. Next, Timmy held Scotty sideways and pressed his paws against one of the whitewashed walls.

"Beautiful!" we agreed as Scotty's paw prints covered the wall.

With the help of a chair, Timmy strained to lift Scotty to the ceiling, where he added more prints.

As a finishing touch, we placed a barbell weight under a small table, where it had been "thrown" across the room.

Then we stepped back to survey the area.

"It sure looks to me like ZoZo was here," I said.

"Me too!" Timmy said.

Scotty looked as though he couldn't wait to get away from these two crazy people.

We returned to the recorder to finish our interview.

"How long will you be staying here?" I asked ZoZo.

"I do not know. I must wait for instructions from my planet. In the meantime, I will continue to observe life on this block."

"Would you be willing to talk to our friends while you are here?" Timmy asked, setting the stage for us to get Pete and M.C.

"I have revealed myself to you so that you can convey the

nature of my mission to others with whom you reside. I may not be speaking to you again."

After ZoZo spoke his final words, we fast-forwarded the tape and shut off the recorder.

"I got a great idea," Timmy said.

Then he shared his thoughts for an appropriate ending for the tape.

A short while later, we headed outside to find Pete and M.C. As luck would have it, they had just finished working out and were sitting on M.C.'s stoop.

"Hey, you guys, how's it going?" I asked.

"Everything is cool," M.C. responded. "What's new with you guys?"

"You guys are never going to believe what just happened!"

"Oh yeah? What?" Pete asked.

"Maybe we'd better talk about it in Timmy's basement," I suggested, looking around in a way that I hoped would generate curiosity about the situation.

Pete and M.C. exchanged puzzled looks, then hopped off the stoop and followed us over to Timmy's house. As Timmy and I walked slightly ahead, we peered at each other with a sense of mischievousness and fought hard to keep straight faces.

When we got to Timmy's basement, Timmy dramatically took one last look around before opening the door to the clubroom and gesturing for everyone to enter. Then he quickly closed it.

With the door safely secured, he spun around.

"Before we tell you guys what happened, you have to swear you won't tell anyone else!"

Pete and M.C. gave each other more puzzled looks.

"What's going on?" M.C. demanded, his tone reflecting a growing frustration with all the cloak-and-dagger secrecy.

"You gotta promise to keep this a secret," I repeated for emphasis.

"Okay, okay," Pete responded impatiently. "What happened?"

Timmy took out the tape recorder, but before turning it on, he pointed to the paw print on top of the dresser.

"See that?" he said, as though it was self-explanatory.

"See what?" M.C. responded with continued annoyance.

"The paw print, dummy!" Timmy replied, as though M.C. should have known what it was.

"What about it?" Pete asked.

"Do you know how it got up there?" I asked, trying to set up what was to follow.

"How should I know?" M.C. growled.

Timmy turned on the recorder and let Pete and M.C. listen for themselves. When the tape was over, there was thirty seconds of silence as M.C. and Pete attempted to digest what they had just heard.

"Do you mean to tell us that Scotty is really some kind of creature from outer space?" Pete asked.

"I know it's crazy," I said. "If I hadn't seen it with my own eyes, I never would have believed it either."

"I'm telling you," Timmy said, "that we saw Scotty or ZoZo—or whatever you want to call him—fly around the room, walk up the walls, stand upside down on the ceiling, and then toss that weight across the room just by thinking about it."

The room fell silent again as M.C. and Pete played Sherlock Holmes and Dr. Watson, examining various pieces of evidence from the unbelievable event.

"This whole thing is a little hard to accept," Pete said as he scrutinized the prints on the ceiling.

M.C., on the other hand, was much more blunt. "How do we know you guys didn't set this whole thing up? How do we know that? Huh?"

"Mario," I said, using M.C.'s Christian name for effect, "see for yourself. There are footprints on top of the dresser! And more on the wall! There are footprints on the ceiling! Whaddaya want? Footprints on your face before you believe us?!"

They still weren't biting. Time to switch tactics.

"Let me ask you something," I said, trying a more reasonable tone. "Don't you think Timmy's mother would have a fit if she saw those paw prints all over this place, and it was just from Scotty running loose?"

M.C. blinked. He and Pete recalled Timmy's mother's behavior during our Bomber Party preparations, and the point about risking her wrath over a prank seemed to hit home. M.C. and then Pete requested another playback of the tape.

They scrutinized each word while Timmy and I avoided eye contact for fear of breaking into laughter.

After two or three more reviews of the tape, we got into a discussion about ZoZo landing in the lumberyard.

"You're right to think that the whole thing is crazy," I said, using reverse psychology. "The only thing I can say is that it really did happen!"

It was farfetched, all right, but we could sense that M.C. and Pete both wanted to believe us. After all, like everyone else on the block, they watched *The Twilight Zone*. Why couldn't it be true?

After another hour of discussion, it was getting late, so Timmy moved to set up Pete and M.C. for the finale. "Before Danny and I came outside to see you, we went upstairs to get some sodas, and we forgot to turn off the tape recorder," he said. "Maybe ZoZo left a message while we were away. Let's play the tape a little longer."

Timmy fast-forwarded the tape to the end and let it resume at normal speed. As we huddled around the recorder, M.C. pressed an ear against the speaker, hearing only the static sound of silence. But after a few minutes, the voice of the alien ZoZo returned.

"I have one final message to communicate to you before I depart your planet."

Without picking up his head, M.C. nudged Pete. "Hey, there he is again! I wonder what the message is."

Then we all heard Porky Pig's closing remarks from the *Looney Tunes Cartoons* as he stammered directly into M.C.'s ear. "Th-th-that's all, folks!"

M.C.'s face turned crimson as he realized that he and Pete had been had. Timmy and I then burst into laughter, knowing our spoof had proven to be... *one small step for aliens and one giant leap for adolescent silliness!*

Chapter IX

Operation Walk Like A Man

The remaining months of winter dragged by slowly, and after an eternity of cold weather, life on the block finally thawed out. Pete and Eileen were still going together, and all seemed well with them, or at least I thought so. As the weather got warmer and the days grew longer, we all got together more often and talked about plans for the summer that seemed just around the corner.

As it turned out, summer wasn't the only thing around the corner that came up for discussion. The more I saw Eileen and Pete together—or not together, as was the case—the more I suspected there might be trouble in paradise. Initially I thought Pete was just shaking things up a little with Eileen. He did that sometimes to keep her on her toes. After a few weeks, however, I surmised there might be more to it, so I got Pete aside one night and asked him what was going on.

"Hey, Pete," I began, "something going on between you and Eileen? I haven't seen you two together lately."

"Dan," he said in a serious tone, "Eileen and I have broken up."

"What? You wanna run that by me again?" I wasn't sure I'd heard him correctly.

"Yeah, we've broken up. There's someone else who I think

I dig, and I want to check her out."

"Who is she? Anyone I know?"

"I don't think so. Her name is Pam. She moved in on Palmetto Street over the winter, and I've seen her a few times at the German deli."

"Does Eileen know about her?"

"Oh yeah, she knows, but she's not happy about it. I want to check things out with Pam to see if I want to make a move with her, and I need your help."

"Sure, just let me know what you need."

The remainder of the night was spent talking about Pam. I was intrigued about what kind of girl would threaten an institution like Pete and Eileen. They had stayed together throughout an entire winter and, for all practical purposes, had acted like they were married.

Near the end of our conversation, we decided to arrange a future game of ring-a-lievio with the kids from Palmetto Street, including Pam. Payoff was considered too risky since Pam might have reservations about making out with someone the first time she showed up on the block. So we agreed that ring-a-lievio was the safest choice. It would give Pete a chance to flirt with Pam within the context of an innocent game while I checked out how she reacted to him. Our plan called for Pete and I to stay close to Pam during the game. If she went after him, it might be a good signal that she was interested. If she went after me, it might be a sign that she wasn't interested in him or that she was playing it cool. Just to be on the safe side, we put the word out about our plan before the game. We had to make sure there was no outside interference.

The night of the game, we waited on Pete's stoop for the Palmetto Street crowd to arrive. When they turned the corner,

Pete nudged me.

"There she is," he whispered, "the one in the middle."

Surrounded by other members of the Palmetto Street crowd, the mystery girl Pam looked like Elizabeth Taylor in *Cleopatra*, protected by her slaves.

I took a long hard look at her. "Hey, she's pretty nice. I wish I saw her first."

Pam had jet-black hair and perfectly clear cream-colored skin. Physically, she was extremely attractive with well-proportioned legs and what looked like nicely developed breasts. As I watched her approach, I felt a little envious, but I promised myself that I would honor the unwritten rule of the block: when a guy declared an intention to make a play for a girl, he had first crack at her without any interference. That is, until it was clear she wasn't interested.

During the ring-a-lievio game, I felt very relaxed knowing that I had nothing at stake. My primary goal was to help Pete find out what he needed to know. Oddly enough, my free and easy style appeared to make me attractive to Pam.

Prior to the game, Pete and I had done a little reconnaissance on Pam and found out that she had a reputation for being a quitter—a girl who went out with guys for only a short while and then dropped them without warning. Pam was hot and had little trouble finding guys who wanted to go out with her. She had gone out with most of the guys from Palmetto Street at least once and some twice. There was even one guy who had dated her three times, and rumor had it he was considering a fourth try!

Based on our observations, we concluded that Pam was attracted to guys who played hard to get. Every time she got near Pete and me, I'd whiz by her, getting close enough to let her reach out and then just miss. When I cut out on her, I found her tearing right behind me. The fact that I didn't care, coupled with my teasing, only seemed to make her more interested.

The next evening, Pete's mother and father went out to dinner, so I headed over for an extensive strategy session. On my way, I passed Palmetto Street and nodded hello to Pam, who was on the corner with some friends. As I continued to the block, I thought again to myself that if Pete hadn't seen her first, I would definitely have made a play for her.

When I arrived at Pete's, he was in the process of laying down the law to his kid brothers—Stephen, James, and Michael—and his younger sister, Margaret, who was the second oldest. While Margaret was rarely a problem, Pete's younger brothers had their moments. Stephen, eight, was jumping off a bunk bed to attack James and Michael. Following several warnings from Pete, Stephen was treated to the latest torture holds from that week's segment of *Saturday Night Wrestling*. Six-year-old James was directed by Pete to shut up or risk the same fate as Stephen. Stephen's cries for mercy convinced James not to press his luck. Through it all, little three-year-old Michael had to stand in a corner and stare at it until it moved. After only a minute or two, he turned to Pete and babbled, "Petey, Petey, I see it moving. I be a good boy now."

Pete showed leniency and sent Michael back to bed.

Then Pete and I got down to the business at hand, discussing the events of the prior evening.

I commended him on his choice of Pam and added that I wished I had seen her first. Pete then stunned me by saying he had done a lot of thinking during the night and had decided not to make a play for her. He added that Eileen was scheduled to join him later that night to "make things up" to him. (Apparently, when Pete's parents were out, and he and I weren't having strategy sessions, Eileen would keep him company while he babysat. Sometimes he would tell Eileen he was tired and then Colleen would come down and keep him company. Needless to say, babysitting was not a major sacrifice for Pete.)

Following Pete's disclosure, the situation with Pam became a brand-new ball game. We briefly talked about her reputation as a quitter and her reaction during the ring-a-lievio game. Considering all these factors, we formulated a strategy to act cool and not play up to her. We code-named our plan "Operation Walk Like A Man" after a popular song released by the Four Seasons the previous winter. While the idea of acting cool toward Pam ran contrary to my feelings, the strategy session with Pete clearly indicated that this was the intelligent course of action. If I had learned anything from the experience with Eileen the year before, it was that if you moved too quickly with a girl in the beginning, it was almost impossible to slow things down later. On the other hand, if you played it slow at first, you could always pick up the pace. So from that night on, whenever I saw Pam, I played it cool, just nodding or saying something like, "Hi, how's it going?" Then I'd nonchalantly keep heading toward Woodbine Street.

The weeks went by and school finally ended. In addition to stickball, the guys started a handball tournament. Those of us from Woodbine Street usually played handball by the garages near Ridgewood Place. For the tournament, however, we used the large smooth brick wall of a new warehouse that had been built on Palmetto Street. Hank, one of the Palmetto Royals, was the reigning champ and had gone undefeated for several weeks.

To play against Hank required participation in an elimination tournament. After a series of matches, I finally got a chance to challenge him for the championship in a best two-out-of-three game series. Inspired by Pam's presence, I crushed Hank in two straight games.

Throughout the match I continued to play it cool with Pam, acting friendly but aloof. While I harbored a burning desire to rush over and tell her how much I dug her, Operation Walk Like a Man seemed to be working. I just needed to stay the course.

Shortly after the handball tournament, word came from Palmetto Street that "Pam liked Danny." My patience had paid off. If I stayed cool a little while longer, I'd be home free and would finally get to go out with a girl I really liked!

Pete and I checked out the rumors to make sure they were solid before I made any moves. Within a few days, we received confirmation from Eileen, who had spoken with a girl named Kathy, who was Pam's best friend on Palmetto Street. Pete and I held several more strategy sessions to decide the all-important matters of where, when, and how I would ask Pam to go out with me. While we weren't quite sure of the details, we agreed that I shouldn't ask her out unless the answer was a guaranteed yes.

My pursuit of Pam was not without challenges. The summer and winter before, I couldn't get any of the girls on Woodbine Street to give me so much as the time of day. When I had liked Eileen, she'd liked Pete. Then, after the Bomber Party, when Eileen went back with Pete, Lisa and Colleen had focused their attention on Timmy. Then Lisa gave up on

Timmy and decided that she liked me, and for a short while, I liked the idea of her liking me. She was a nice girl, and although her weight had continued to be an issue for me, I'd asked her out several times over the winter. We'd gone out for short intervals of a day or two, with the longest stretch going six days due to a heavy exam schedule that had kept us apart.

When Pam entered the scene, Lisa tried to get her to stay clear of me, but Lisa's efforts only seemed to make Pam more determined.

Pete and I continued to test the waters with Pam through Eileen, who arranged to run into Kathy during trips to the German deli on the corner of Pam's block. Eileen was instructed to strike up conversations with Kathy and let her know that I might ask Pam out if I could be sure she'd say yes. Over the next few days, word from Eileen was very encouraging. She was not only pleased for me but also happy that she could stop going to the deli so often.

At the beginning of July, we moved into the final phase of Operation Walk Like A Man.

The final major hurdle involved getting Pam alone because she was often watching her younger siblings. At other times she was also surrounded by Palmetto Street guys, who hung around and hoped to be her next boyfriend.

Pete and I settled on a target date of the Fourth of July for me to pop the question. Late that afternoon I made a brief appearance on Palmetto Street to check things out. Unfortunately, due to the holiday fireworks, there was too much going on, so I postponed my move till the next day. Before leaving, I told Pam I hoped to see her the following evening. Rather than return to Woodbine Street, I went straight home. The next day, though, I heard from Eileen that

Pam and Kathy had stopped around, apparently looking for me on the Fourth after I had gone home.

July 5 came, but Pam had to stay home and watch the kids. Her mother and father were divorced, and I got the impression that she got stuck with a lot of childcare responsibilities.

So it looked like I would now pop the question on July 6.

During that day, I played stickball, then headed to Bushwick High, where a summer recreation program had just begun. Unfortunately, Pete had started a summer job and wasn't around. Eileen and I discussed the Pam situation over a couple games of bumper pool. She was almost certain that Pam would say yes if I asked her to go out with me. We both agreed that if the opportunity presented itself, I would make my move that night.

That evening, I arrived on the block at my usual time of six thirty. As I passed Palmetto Street, I checked to see if Pam was around, but I only saw Kathy. I stopped to say hello and began to lay the groundwork for the evening. Kathy knew what was up and grinned from ear to ear. I asked her if Pam would be out later, and she assured me that she would be. "Good," I said, "because I have something I want to ask her."

The air was thick with teenage drama!

I hoped that Kathy would rush to Pam and make sure she was outside when I returned. When I came back, butterflies filled my stomach because all the time spent on strategic planning boiled down to the next few hours. I had a lot invested and wanted everything to go as planned.

At precisely 7:45 p.m., I headed around to Palmetto Street to make my move. A month and a half of strategy sessions rested on the next half hour. Eileen and Pete had wished me well, and I agreed to let them know how things worked out. I hopped off Pete's stoop, checked myself out one last time in the side mirror of a parked car, popped a peppermint Life Saver into my mouth, and headed over.

Upon arriving, I spotted Pam and Kathy talking to some of the others from their crowd. When Pam saw me, her face lit up and her eyes acknowledged my presence. I headed over and made small talk. Kathy knew what was coming and beamed. She gradually ushered the crowd away from us, giving me a chance to be alone with Pam.

After discussing preliminary, nonrelevant things, I steered the conversation to the subject at hand. "I've heard some rumors floating around about you and me and was wondering if they might be true."

"What have you heard?" she replied coyly.

Not wanting to beat around the bush, I became more direct. "I've heard that you like me and that I might feel the same way about you. But these are only rumors, and now that you and I are here alone, we can talk straight with each other. I want you to know that the rumors about my digging you are true, and I'd also like to know if you'll go out with me."

There, I'd said it, and the moment of truth had arrived. I took a slow breath after popping the question.

Pam leaned against the wall of our handball building and stared down at her sneakers. She responded without picking up her head. "I don't know. Right now, I need some time to think it over."

I was shocked and more than slightly annoyed! After all the discussions that had taken place between her girlfriend Kathy and Eileen, the last answer I expected to hear was, *I don't know.*

Despite Pam's reputation, Pete and I had figured she'd play

it differently this time, but she apparently had other ideas. I decided not to play her game and pressed for an immediate answer.

"What's there to think about? You either know you want to go out with me or you don't."

She continued to play it cool and again responded that she needed time to think about how she felt.

A few days earlier when I had talked to my older brother about this possibility, he told me that if a girl said she had to think things over, I should tell her to take a walk. Remembering this, I took a firm position. "If you need time, then maybe I've been mistaken, and the rumors aren't true. I guess it pays never to listen to rumors anyway. Let's just forget I asked."

Pam kept her head down and said she understood. She headed to her house, and I returned to Woodbine Street.

When I turned the corner, Eileen and Pete were no longer on their stoop. I rang Pete's doorbell, and he came out into his hall and asked me how things went. When I told him, he became as angry as I was. He called Eileen down and ripped into her as though it were all her fault, saying she must have gotten the wrong signals from Pam's friend Kathy. Eileen swore up and down that Kathy had said Pam would say yes, and if I didn't believe her, I should talk to Kathy myself. I assured her that I believed her and that I'd take her up on the suggestion to talk to Kathy.

As luck would have it, I ran into Kathy that night as I headed home. When she spotted me, she broke into a big grin. The grin melted, however, when we got closer and she saw the angry expression on my face.

"Have you spoken to Pam yet?" she asked.

"Oh yeah, I've spoken to her, but I'm not happy with what she had to say."

"What do you mean?"

I explained, and Kathy acted truly upset. She told me that perhaps there had been a misunderstanding and that if I wanted her to, she would talk to Pam. I figured I had nothing to lose, so I gave her the okay. As Kathy ran off to talk to Pam, I headed back to Pete's house to update him. He suggested I take some time to sleep on things. I agreed and then headed back home.

On my way, I bumped into Kathy again as she was returning from Pam's house. She explained that Pam needed some time because she didn't want to appear too eager by saying yes right after I asked her. I let go of my sense of annoyance. Then I instructed Kathy to tell Pam that I understood and to let her know that my original offer was open. Kathy broke into her famous grin and raced back to Pam's house. Two minutes later she came running back to catch up with me, and in an excited voice—half out of breath—she told me that Pam had reconsidered, and the answer was yes!

It was music to my ears.

I thanked Kathy for her assistance and then excitedly returned to Pete's house yet again to fill him in on the good news. After I rang the bell a few times, Pete appeared in his hallway looking half-asleep.

"Guess who's going out with you-know-who?" I said, barely concealing my grin.

Pete just looked at me, broke into a smile, and said, "All Right," while slapping me five.

It was late and I was tired. I told Pete I'd fill him in the next day, then I headed home for the third and final time that evening.

Along the way, I whistled up a storm and felt like I was on cloud nine.

In bed that night, I tucked my arms under my pillow and thought about all the strategy sessions that had led to the success of Operation Walk Like A Man.

Overtaken by sleep, I whispered to myself, "Pam and Danny."

Way to go!

Chapter X

Going Out

In the fifties it was called "going steady." For us it was known as "going out," which meant that a guy and girl had made a commitment to each other, and neither was available to date anyone else unless, that is, they cheated or broke up. Around Woodbine and Palmetto Streets, everyone knew everybody else, and cheating on your boyfriend or girlfriend was like cheating on the entire crowd—an offense punishable by expulsion.

While the length of time that people went out varied, there were very few steady relationships that lasted a long time. Except for Pete and Eileen, who'd been going out for close to a year, going out usually lasted anywhere from a week to a month. During the summer, when everyone saw each other daily, steady relationships tended to be shorter. People got bored with each other or became attracted to more than one person at a time. Our sense of time was also different during the summer. The days started early, ended late, and were packed with lots of action in between. Two months of summer vacation contained more experiences than the rest of the year combined and spending an entire school vacation tied down to one person was almost unthinkable.

Around the neighborhood, when a guy met a girl and

wanted to know if she was available, all he had to do was to check how she tied the laces on her sneakers. If the laces were tied at the bottom, it meant she was going out with someone and was off-limits. If, on the other hand, both laces were tied at the top, it meant the girl was neither going out with anyone nor interested in doing so. This usually happened if she had just broken up with someone and wanted time off before getting involved again. Lastly, if one lace was tied at the top and the other at the bottom, she was available.

The day after I asked Pam to go out with me, I woke up early and was floating on air. The sun was shining brightly, and birds were singing on the fire escape outside our kitchen window. All was right with the world, and not even my brother's taunts of "skanky Pam looks like a ham" could bother me.

While I was brushing my teeth, a song called "So Much in Love" by a new group called the TYMES came over the radio and described exactly how I felt.

As soon as I heard it, I knew I had to have it before heading to the block. I rushed out to buy it, but the record and group were so new that the local record stores hadn't even heard of it yet. To my satisfaction, however, "So Much in Love" was selected as the Pick Hit of the Week several weeks later and eventually became the number one song on all the stations.

After my unsuccessful record search, I headed to Palmetto Street to see Pam. She usually didn't come out until eleven, so I went around to Woodbine Street, where I got into a game of stickball and received congratulations from the guys on the block. Word of my going out with Pam had already spread like wildfire.

At eleven thirty, I strolled to the German deli to get a soda and check if Pam was out. Upon leaving the store, I spotted her across the street, and she saw me at the same time. Our eyes locked, and the lyrics from "So Much in Love" played in my head. Unfortunately, Pam was not alone, as a few of her younger siblings and some of the Palmetto Street crowd were hanging around. I crossed over to say hello, and we held a brief conversation over the muffled giggles from the young kids on a nearby stoop.

This was first day we were going out together, and I felt a little awkward. I had never gone out with someone I liked as much as Pam, and I wanted to play it cool and not come across too strong. Just because we were going out didn't mean we would be kissy-huggy right away. We still needed time to get to know each other, and for the time being, it was okay for us just to hang out together. As we talked, I glanced down to see if she had retied her laces and was surprised to see that one lace was tied at the bottom while the other remained tied at the top. Rather than speak to her about this directly, I mentioned it to Kathy afterward. Later on, I was pleased to see Pam's laces retied at the bottom, which made our relationship feel official.

Over the next couple of days, I played it cool. The third day was especially important because Pam had never gone out with anyone longer than that. When we made it past that milestone, I felt more confident and relaxed, and I looked forward to moving things along in the making-out department. Up until then, we had not made out or even kissed. A big part of the problem was finding the right time and place. Making out was a private matter, not usually done in public. When Pete and Eileen made out, if he wasn't babysitting, they went off the block to a railroad yard a few blocks away. Getting Pam away from Palmetto Street, however, would not be easy.

She was often babysitting or was surrounded by members of the crowd who weren't wise enough to take the numerous hints I dropped about wanting to be alone with her. Though it seemed appropriate to play it slow at first, it didn't seem unreasonable to expect more than just holding hands.

A week later, I decided to make my move. Pam and I were talking on Palmetto Street with only a few others around.

"Pam," I said, "how about you and I taking a walk?"

"Where to?"

"Oh, you know, just around." I hoped she would read between the lines.

"Why can't we stay here?"

"Because there's too much light here!" I countered, barely concealing my frustration.

Then we got down to the real reason for the walk, and she became more forthcoming for her reason to stay.

"The kids will notice if I'm not around when they come looking for me."

"Don't worry," I said. "We'll be back soon."

"I don't want to take a chance. I have to go home pretty soon anyway."

Five minutes of silence followed as we leaned against the warehouse wall and stared at our sneakers while I rested my arm around her shoulder. My mind raced as I tried to figure out my next move. Finally, one of her kid brothers came to tell her it was time to go in. As he walked ahead of us, I stopped her for a split second and kissed her good night on the lips. It wasn't the same as making out, but at least it was a start!

In mid-July, little Ralphie and his family moved from Woodbine Street to the suburbs in Brentwood, Long Island. We all wished him well, and in tribute to him, we painted his number on the ground near home plate—our version of the major-league practice of retiring the number of famous ball players. With the loss of Ralphie to the suburbs and Pete to his part-time job, the rivalry between the Royals and the Bombers lost its intensity, and we played stickball less frequently. Most of the action shifted to the gymnasium of Bushwick High across the street from the block, where a summer recreation program was in full swing.

At the recreation program, there were lots of things to do during the day: basketball, ping-pong, bumper pool, Wiffle ball, and swimming in the new pool. The program became a magnet for kids from all races of the neighborhood: Black, White, and Puerto Rican. For all of the neighborhood kids attending the center, racial tensions reported in the newspapers and on television got lost in our pursuit of the perfect hook shot or beating each other in ping-pong.

At the gym we became friendly with one of the counselors, a Jewish guy named Stan Harris in his last year of dental school. Stan was younger than the other counselors and the only one who wasn't a teacher. We connected with him in a different way and shared with him some of the inner workings of the crowd. In return, he opened us up to new things, like gymnastics, and spent a lot of time teaching us assorted moves on the parallel bars.

Throughout this time, I saw Pam on an on-again, off-again basis. Sometimes she'd come over to the gym, and other times she'd stay on Palmetto Street. Given her history of quitting guys she went out with, I was beginning to wonder how much longer we would last. In addition to my frustration about wanting to make out with her or even just spend time with her alone, I was also struggling with Mother Nature and the fact that my face was breaking out in acne.

My burgeoning skin problem significantly affected the way I felt about myself and how I related to Pam. On days when my face looked okay, I felt confident and was more outgoing. But on days when my face was broken out badly, I withdrew and grew self-conscious. Some of the popular lotions offered temporary relief but were no match for hormone changes and constant sweating in the hot weather. As a result, on bad-skin days, I communicated with Pam through intermediaries, mainly Kathy. From the beginning of our relationship, Pam seemed to have problems communicating directly with me, and as a result, she too used Kathy to convey messages. It got to a point where I felt like I was going out with Kathy more than I was with Pam.

Gradually, the lack of direct communication, my feelings about my complexion, and concerns about Pam's history as a quitter took their toll on our relationship. The longer we went out, the more inevitable it became that Pam would be calling it quits and, in doing so, adding me to her list of "formers." So despite the fact that I still liked her a lot—even more since we had first started going out—I debated whether I should call it quits with her first, a decision I struggled with. Unlike the problems between Pete and Eileen, which were easier for me to see because I wasn't directly involved, the situation with Pam was totally different and my options not so clear-cut. At times I'd have my mind all made up to break off with her, but after seeing her, especially when she looked good, I'd have a change of heart.

Eventually, after going out together for three weeks, I decided to call it quits. So one day as I was walking to the gym, I ran into her alone and told her I wanted to talk. She seemed happy to see me and probably didn't expect what was coming. Rather than change my mind again, I got straight to the point. "Pam, I think it's over between us. I want to call it quits."

She looked surprised and sad, then did an abrupt about-face and ran back to Palmetto Street. I continued toward the gym, already regretting what I had done. When I got there, I told Eileen what had happened. She was sorry to hear it. Then I went on to tell her I wasn't sure I had done the right thing. Later, when Pete got home from work, I talked to him about it and told him I was having second thoughts. By then, however, I didn't want to use any new strategies. I just wanted to go around to Palmetto Street, tell Pam it was all a bad mistake, and get her to go back with me. But that would put Pam squarely in the driver's seat, so I spoke to Kathy, who offered little sympathy or help. She was angry that I had broken up with her best friend, especially after all the trouble she had gone through to get us together.

I let things cool down for the next few days and spent most of the time at Bushwick. The weather had shifted from hot and sunny to cloudy with intermittent showers. On the rainy days, the girls brought their record player and 45s to the gym and danced while the guys played basketball or ping-pong. The Waddle was the big dance at the time, and the most popular song was "My Boyfriend's Back" by a new female group called the Angels. It always seemed that whenever Pam was already at the gym, that song would play when I arrived. Despite my efforts to patch things up, it became apparent that our getting back together was not meant to be. Sometimes when she came to the gym and danced with the girls, I'd throw her glances while playing ball, and she'd return them while dancing the Waddle. I still thought she looked good, although I had discovered one flaw: a large cavity in her front tooth. Stan told me that if she didn't take care of that tooth soon, she wouldn't be looking so hot later, a fact I made a note of since he was studying to be a dentist.

Since Pete was not around, I talked strategy with Stan. He was very understanding and didn't minimize my feelings because I was a kid. His advice was that if Pam still didn't want to go back with me after all my attempts, I should tell her a Yiddish expression that meant that she should kiss my butt. While this made sense in my head, it was hard for me to accept in my heart.

The final blow to any chances of a reconciliation came in mid-August when a new guy named Nicky appeared on the scene. He lived a few blocks away and was brought around by a guy on Palmetto Street who went to school with him. Nicky was an olive-skinned, good-looking Italian kid, but not very swift. Shortly after his arrival, rumors spread hot and heavy that Pam liked Nicky. Stan and my friends from the block speculated that Pam may have started the rumor to get me jealous. While it bothered me, I followed Stan's counsel to wait and see how quickly Pam could get Nicky to ask her out. In almost no time at all, Stan was proven right. A few days after the rumor started, word got out that Nicky had fallen for her and had already asked her to go out.

To get over Pam, I got heavily involved in an end-of-summer sports tournament sponsored by the recreation center. With Pete working, my main competition came from M.C., Davey from the Palmetto Royals, a Spanish guy named Bobby (who was going out with Colleen), and Pam's new boyfriend, Nicky. Timmy also occasionally came to the gym, but he spent most of that summer training his dog, Scotty, aka ZoZo. Richie also didn't come around much because he had to work at his family's restaurant.

During the track competition of the tournament, Davey won the half-mile race, and I was able to salvage second with a sprinting finish. In basketball, Bobby won the foul-shooting contest, and Eileen picked up a gold medal in bumper pool. When we got to ping-pong, the final match for the medal came down to Nicky and me. Nicky had beaten me a few times prior to the tournament and was acting as though he had the medal clinched, which only added fuel to the fire that still burned inside me about Pam.

Several days before our final match, I practiced and talked with Stan. In college, Stan had played football, and he told me that smart teams never gave the competition a reason to want to beat them, e.g., by bragging, like Nicky had done. As we practiced, Stan also reinforced that "a good defense is a good offense!" That is, I shouldn't let my emotions over Nicky and Pam make me play too aggressively and thereby make mistakes. Instead, by playing good defense, I might force Nicky to make mistakes.

When the day of the big match arrived, I made a point of remembering Stan's advice. We were to play a twenty-one-point game, with the winner required to win by two points if we tied at twenty, which is exactly what happened. When the game went into overtime, other events at the gym came to a halt as everyone crowded the pullout bleachers near the ping-pong table. Stan and my friends from the block had all been there from the start, sitting down front where I could feel their supportive presence. The Palmetto Street crowd was also there, including Pam, who sat in front on Nicky's side of the table.

I did my best to block out her presence, and every time Nicky slammed the ball over the net, I would calmly return it to the middle of his side. When we were in quadruple overtime, Nicky seemed frustrated and tried unsuccessfully to slam return shots to my side edge. Finally, when his last attempted slam shot unsuccessfully flew off to the side—nowhere near the table—the B Girls let out a loud roar.

The victory and gold medal were mine!

I had just become the Bushwick Recreation Center Ping-Pong Champion of 1963!

Not only had I beaten Nicky for the first time and won the medal, but the victory was made sweeter by the fact that Pam had been rooting for him from the sidelines. When he missed the last point, Nicky threw his paddle to the floor and stormed out of the gym, causing many in the bleachers to boo him for his unsportsmanlike behavior. Pam, sensing the crowd's hostility, quickly fled and ran after him.

Pam's behavior during the match, followed by her scurrying after Nicky, caused me to lose any remaining desire I had to get back with her.

After Nicky and Pam left, I went over to Stan, who shook my hand and placed his other hand on my shoulder as he smiled and said, "Well done! You played a smart game." I grinned from ear to ear and thanked him for his words of wisdom and encouragement.

The next day I was back in the recreation center practicing gymnastics moves Stan had shown me on the parallel bars. When Eileen spotted me, she ran over with an excited look on her face.

"Danny, guess what I just heard from Kathy?"

"Let me guess. Pam broke up with Nicky."

"Yes, but that's not all. Kathy said that Pam wants to get back together with you and will say yes if you ask her out again. What are you going to do?"

"Yeah, what *are* you going to do?" Stan echoed.

"Well," I said, "I think I am going to get myself a Devil Dog and soda to celebrate my big win, my good friends, and a wise recreation counselor!"

I hopped off the parallel bars, slapped Stan five, and gave Eileen a hug for being such a good friend.

When I left the gym and walked down the ramp that led to the sidewalk, I heard "Walk Like A Man" blasting from the radio of passing car. I stopped for a moment and reflected on my experiences with Pam and what I had learned about going out with her and about life. As the car pulled away and the song faded into the distance, I straightened up and walked like a man away from Pam and the summer of 1963!

Chapter XI

Ups and Downs

Two days later marked the last session of Bushwick's recreation program and the end of another summer of growing and learning. After watching the March on Washington and listening to Martin Luther King's "I Have a Dream" speech, I went over to say so long to Stan, who, in Pete's absence, had been my reliable confidant and had provided me with wise counsel.

Stan was heading back to his final year of dental school, and for many of us on the block, the fall of 1963 brought prospects of starting new schools. The Twins, M.C., and Timmy were all attending Bushwick, and I was entering Brooklyn Tech. Pete was already in his junior year at Thomas Edison Vocational High in Queens, where he was studying plumbing. Lisa, on the other hand, had unfortunately gotten left back and had to repeat a year at St. Brigid's. She wound up getting teased a lot about still having to wear her green plaid uniform and white saddle shoes to school.

For the Twins, M.C., and Timmy, Bushwick meant they could literally fall out of bed and walk across the street to school. For me, Brooklyn Tech represented a major step toward realizing a childhood dream I'd held since fifth grade, which was to become an electrical engineer. Back then I thought electrical engineers were the guys who drove trains, and since I enjoyed playing with my Lionel trains at Christmas, I figured that was what I wanted to be. As I got older, I learned that electrical engineers were *not* the guys who drove trains. In junior high, I took electrical shop and felt encouraged by my successes in repairing toasters, irons, and other "sophisticated" devices. I also became more interested in electricity and electronics, and learned that electrical engineers made good salaries, wore suits and ties, and worked in nice offices with attractive secretaries. I especially enjoyed the reactions from strangers when they asked me what I wanted to be when I grew up, and I told them, "An electrical engineer!"

Throughout my public-school education, I had the good fortune of having teachers who encouraged me to aim high in pursuing my dreams, including attending college—something no one else in my family had done.

Most everyone else in the neighborhood had no plans to attend college. Upon graduating high school, guys usually took civil service or blue-collar jobs, and girls became secretaries until they got married and had children. In junior high, when the time came to select a high school, my guidance counselor strongly recommended Brooklyn Tech. After reading several brochures on the school, I was convinced it was the place for me. Tech was one of the more prestigious special public high schools in the city and required passing an entrance exam to be admitted. The first time I went to Tech to take the exam, I was overwhelmed by the school's size and sense of tradition. The auditorium seated over three thousand people and was one of the largest in the city, second only to Radio City Music Hall. The student body numbered nearly six thousand, and the building, with a huge radio antenna on its roof, spanned almost an entire city block.

When I learned I had passed the exam and was accepted, I immediately had mixed feelings. On the one hand, I had taken a major step toward achieving my dream, but on the other, I would be entering the academic big leagues because Tech's national reputation meant classes with some of the smartest kids from all over New York City. Additionally, Tech was located some distance from where I lived. Although this had also been the case with my commute to junior high, I'd traveled back and forth with Timmy during my last year there, which had provided a link between school and my life on the block. Now I'd be going to Tech by myself, and the extent of the relationships I formed there would last for the length of the school day but not much beyond that. Also, Tech was an all-boys school, so there'd be no possibility of meeting new girls.

My first week at Tech was exciting. I purchased all sorts of patches for my jackets as well as covers for my books, announcing that I was a "TECH ENGINEER." As soon as I could, I placed an order for a Tech winter jacket. It was made of blue wool, with white satin stripes running down each sleeve and "TECH" spelled out in large white letters on the back. I could hardly wait for cold weather to arrive so I could wear it.

I was also psyched about my classes. In addition to the usual subjects like Math, English, and Social Studies, I took Mechanical Drawing, Pattern-Making Shop, and Industrial Processes. My enthusiasm far outweighed the hazing I received from upperclassmen who taunted me about being a "froshy" as they offered to sell me bogus passes to the school's elevator.

After a few weeks, I got into the swing of things

academically. Additionally, because of my positive experience on the parallel bars at Bushwick, I joined Tech's gymnastics team. All the uncertainty I'd felt at the start of the academic year began to ease, and I even learned new routines on the high bar.

In late September, while my workload was still manageable, I spent two nights a week at Bushwick's night center. As the weather turned cooler, those visits gave me opportunities to wear the jackets I had sewn Tech patches onto. I spent most of my time there practicing new high-bar moves I'd learned on the Tech team. I figured that if I practiced enough, I might earn a letter in gymnastics, which I could wear on my new Tech winter jacket.

I often practiced at Bushwick with an older guy named Ronnie, who was on their varsity gym team. He helped me with numerous routines and showed me new ones as well. One of the moves I particularly liked was a complicated dismount that involved hanging by the legs, swinging back, letting go, and then landing upright on the mat. Ronnie spotted me when I tried it, and although I missed a few times, he was there to break my fall until I got the "hang" of it.

As October approached, the focus of attention on the block turned to the World Series, which brought with it a matchup of old New York rivals: THE DODGERS vs. THE YANKEES!!!

The previous summer, there had been countless debates on the library steps about what might happen if sluggers like Mickey Mantle and Roger Maris of the Yankees met Sandy Koufax and Don Drysdale, the ace pitchers of the Dodgers. When I was younger, my father had taken my brother and me to watch the Dodgers at Ebbets Field, where we saw a doubleheader against the St. Louis Cardinals. My favorite player was Duke Snider, so for Christmas one year, I received a Duke Snider model baseball glove, which had become old and worn over the years—perfect for stickball.

Although the Dodgers moved to California in 1957 and Duke Snider was in the twilight of his career with the Mets, my father and I remained loyal Dodgers fans. All summer long, I singlehandedly engaged in verbal combat with the diehard Yankees fans on the block who bragged about how "Mickey would eat up Sandy like he was candy" or how "Roger would make Drysdale Goodbyes-dale." Now the World Series would settle the debates once and for all.

In 1963, all the World Series games were played during the day, so the Series was the main topic of discussion during our school lunch period. Between sixth and seventh periods in the afternoon, we also tried to get updates on scores from our small transistor radios. Realizing the impact of the games on our attention span, some of the more enlightened teachers posted scores when we entered their classrooms. At the end of the eighth and final period, we returned to our homerooms and tried to catch some of the action on the radio before heading home. If the train ran on schedule, I could arrive home in time to watch some of the games on television, but I declined to do so because I had a superstitious feeling that watching might jinx the Dodgers. So I confined myself to waiting to learn the score on the evening television news or in the early edition of the next day's newspapers.

In the first game of the series, the Dodgers' ace lefty, Sandy Koufax, set a new World Series record by striking out fifteen Yankees—and at Yankee Stadium, to add insult to injury. While this quieted some of the Yankees fans on the block, I still heard excuses:

"It's just first-game luck."

"Koufax is supposed to be the Dodgers' best pitcher, so what's the big deal?"

"This'll probably be the only game the Dodgers win anyway! Let's see what happens in the second game!"

In the second game, the Dodgers got "lucky" again and beat the Yankees by a score of 4–1. Johnny Podres, another lefty Dodger, was the winning pitcher with some late-inning help from Ron Perranoski. Now the Dodgers were up two games to none in the best-of-seven series.

Despite their continued setbacks, the Yankees fans in the crowd remained cocky and confident.

"Luck-eee," they repeated. "The Yanks are just off to a slow start, that's all! Wait until they get going. Game three will be a different story. You'll see! When Mantle and Maris get ahold of Drysdale out in Dodger stadium, look out!"

The third game was at Dodger stadium in California, and Don Drysdale, a big right-handed pitcher, started for the Dodgers. Unlike the first two games when the Yankees faced lefties, now they were up against a right-hander. A fundamental rule in baseball is that hitters have better odds against opposite-handed pitchers, e.g., right-handed hitters do better against left-handed pitchers, and vice versa. For the Yankees this meant that left-handed power hitters like Mantle and Maris would likely do much better against Drysdale, so Pete and the others felt that this was the game where the Yankees would make their move.

As it turned out, the only moving the Yankees did was walking back to their dugout after they struck out. Drysdale beat them 1–0, the only shutout of the series. More significantly, however, the win put the Dodgers up three games to none, and no team in baseball history had ever won the World Series after losing the first three games.

The situation looked bleak for the diehard Yankees fans on the block. While they resigned themselves to the likelihood of the Yankees not winning the series, they refused to throw in the towel. Their last hope was that the Yankees would not be swept in four games straight, something that had happened only four times in the history of the World Series!

"No way will the Yanks get shut out," M.C. argued. "They ain't dead yet! You'll see! The Yanks may even come back to be the first team to ever win the series after being down three games to none!"

I played it cool and decided not to argue. The Dodgers were sitting pretty, and it looked like my strategy of not watching them on television was paying off. One more game—just one more—and the series would be mine.

Let's go, Dodgers!

The fourth game also took place out in Los Angeles. It was a Sunday afternoon, and since the Dodgers had a big lead in the series, I relaxed a little and decided to watch the game on television with my father. The pitching matchups were a repeat of the first game: Koufax for the Dodgers and Whitey Ford for the Yankees. It promised to be a good one. We settled down on the living room couch, and I put some sixteen-ounce sodas on ice to see me through the game.

So what if the Dodgers had deserted New York? As far as my father and I were concerned, they were still the "Brooklyn Bums" and always would be. For two old loyal Dodgers fans like my father and me, there were few things in the world more important than beating the Yankees in the World Series.

As we sat together on our sofa, I clutched my old Duke

Snider glove for luck.

Finally, it happened.

On October 6, 1963, a date that is etched in my heart forever, my father and I watched Sandy Koufax and the rest of our heroes beat the Yankees 2–1!

After the final out of the game, Johnny Roseboro, the Dodgers' catcher, ran out to the pitcher's mound and hoisted Sandy Koufax into the air.

They had done it!

The Dodgers had swept the Yankees in four straight!

The Dodgers—my Dodgers—were the World Champions!

That evening I went over to the night center at Bushwick to work out and accept congratulations on the Dodgers' victory. Perched atop the high bar, I held court as Pete, M.C., and others in the gym begrudgingly paid homage to the new champions of baseball. Afterward, inspired by the Dodgers' triumph, I tried a new dismount from the high bar, even though there was no one around to catch me if I fell.

The first two times I tried, I fell short and landed forward on my knees. Annoyed at my inability to perform the dismount correctly, I reprimanded myself as I lay on the mat.

"C'mon, Danny!" I said aloud. "If the Dodgers can beat the Yankees, you can do this dismount. Now let's do it right!"

The next time I attempted the dismount, I overcompensated and fell backward.

Hard.

Very hard.

I landed squarely on my right wrist with all my weight, and when I got up from the mat, I felt a slight twinge in my wrist. I glanced at it and could hardly believe my eyes. The impact of the fall had snapped it into the shape of a Z.

This must be a bad dream, I thought. *I'm going to wake up, find myself in bed, and my wrist will be okay.*

After a few seconds, I realized it wasn't a dream.

Then I panicked.

"My wrist! My wrist!" I screamed as I ran over to the teacher in charge of the night center. He took one look at my wrist and rolled his eyes as if to say, What the hell did you do?

He tried to calm me down, took me into a nearby office, and asked me for my telephone number. Since my father was working, it meant that my mother would be called.

Just what I needed.

My mother was never the calmest person under normal circumstances, and during a crisis she was terrible. Whenever there was a family emergency, she became hysterical and more of a problem than the actual problem. Luckily, she was being visited by my Aunt Margie, the unofficial family nurse and the person my brother and I called when we got hurt. When my aunt answered the phone, I explained the situation. Then I briefly spoke to my mother to calm her down and reassure her that I was still alive and well. As soon as I got off the phone, I broke down crying. Not only was I upset about the wrist and my mother's anticipated reaction, but I suddenly felt panicked over how I would complete my schoolwork.

Would this mean I'd have to leave Tech and give up my dream of becoming an electrical engineer?

The recreation center teacher tried to calm me down as he handed me a pile of forms to sign.

"Don't worry, don't worry," he counseled. "You can do your homework left-handed. Here. You can practice writing on these."

I felt like I was back in the first grade as I tried in vain to scribble my name. When my mother arrived, it appeared that my aunt had gotten her under control. To minimize her shock over my wrist, I hid it under my jacket and showed it to her a little at a time. Ten minutes later an ambulance arrived to take me to Wycoff Heights Hospital nearby. Though I felt a little light-headed, I declined to be carried out on a stretcher. The gang from the block would be at the end of the ramp leading from the night center, and I planned on walking into the ambulance under my own power.

I wiped the tears away and threw my jacket, complete with its Tech patch, over my shattered wrist. Slowly, I headed down the ramp. When I reached the ambulance, the gang huddled around with expressions of concern etched on their faces.

"Hey, what happened?"

"Danny, you okay?"

"What's going on?"

I responded with a thumbs-up sign as I walked past them and stepped into the ambulance.

The crowd showed up again at the hospital to keep me company as I waited for X-rays. After three hours in the emergency room, a doctor with a heavy foreign accent came out into the waiting room.

"Your vist is bwoken in thvee pwaces," he reported.

"Great doctor," M.C. mumbled. "We're waiting here three hours, and now he tells us your wrist is broken. I could have told him that before."

The others urged M.C. to be quiet. It was getting late and the gang had to head back home. I thanked them for keeping me company. As they filed out of the waiting area, I headed into an examination room. After a couple of injections in my arm, the twinge subsided. I watched nonchalantly as the doctor straightened my wrist into place with a snap, crackle, and pop, then set it in a cast that extended beyond my elbow. By the end of the first week, the cast was covered with signatures from both the Woodbine Street gang and some new friends from school. For the next six weeks, it would be my constant companion. During that time, I developed an appreciation for everyday tasks that I had taken for granted when I had the use of both hands. Simple things like pouring sugar onto a spoon now had to be broken down into steps that could be performed with one hand. Schoolwork also took much longer, and even though I started my homework as soon as I arrived home, I sometimes didn't finish until after midnight.

Gradually, I adjusted to my situation and realized with relief that my broken wrist wasn't going to force me to leave Tech. I developed a knack for using my left hand more and was able to do most of my homework on time. I even developed a good left-handed game of ping-pong. Despite these adjustments, the weeks dragged by, and I eagerly looked forward to the day my plaster albatross would be removed. At the end of four weeks, my arm and wrist became unbearably itchy, a positive sign that the injury was healing. In mechanical drawing class, I used rulers and compasses to scratch the itch. Sometimes I was successful, but other times the itchy spot was impossible to reach; I thought I'd go out of my mind. By mid-November I had worn the cast for five weeks and had one more week to go. My cast had gotten pretty dirty, and when my family was painting our living room, I decided to spruce the cast up with some light-blue latex paint that had just come on the market.

At school I was holding my own academically, except in

plane geometry, where my grades were suffering. My math teacher announced an exam for that next Friday, the 22nd, that would be in a short-answer, multiple-choice format. I had a strong suspicion the format was for my benefit. To take full advantage of the opportunity, I began studying immediately.

The day before the exam, I went to the family doctor for my weekly checkup. To my pleasant surprise, he said the cast could come off. From his back office, he retrieved a small surgical saw to remove it. As I waited, I looked at the cast one last time and tried to recall what life had been like without it. Fifteen minutes later, it was off, and I was a free man. But my wrist and arm appeared much thinner, and I could only partially straighten my arm. I felt like the Tin Man, whose joints had stiffened without his oil can in *The Wizard of Oz*. My doctor told me not to worry and assured me that in time my arm would straighten back to its original position. He also instructed me to perform exercises, like squeezing a rubber ball to strengthen the muscles in the wrist and hand.

I was happy to see my good ole wrist again that day. It also happened to be my brother's seventeenth birthday and Pete's sixteenth. It felt good to know that I'd be able to have a piece of birthday cake without having to juggle the plate.

As soon as I got home, there was a small party for my brother. After that, I hit the books to prepare for the next day's plane geometry exam. If I flunked, there would be no excuses.

The next day started out well. It was Friday, the weather was clear and cool, and the next week had only three days of school because of the Thanksgiving holiday. In addition, it felt extra good to go to school without my cast. Though I had little mobility in my wrist and arm, it was good to know that the itchy spots that had driven me mad were now out in the open where I could reach them. When I arrived at school, everyone congratulated me on my newly regained freedom. I felt like I had come through a tough time and was better for it.

During lunch period, I quickly ate and then went over my notes for the exam that was scheduled for the eighth and last period of school.

At 2:00 p.m., the exam began.

I anxiously scanned the test paper and immediately worked on those questions that appeared easiest to answer. Fifteen minutes in, chimes rang over the school's public-address system; they usually preceded an announcement.

Seriously? Now? I was annoyed because I felt I had a good chance to write the required lengthy proofs on time, and this exam was an opportunity to significantly improve my math average. Last thing I needed was to waste time listening to some stupid announcement.

The voice of Mr. Pabst, our school principal, came through the speaker. "Attention, all students and faculty, I have an important announcement. We have just received news that President Kennedy has been shot in Dallas. There are no further details at this time."

A hushed silence fell over the classroom.

My initial thought was that the situation with the president probably wasn't anything serious. Perhaps he had been shot in the arm or something minor like that. In my mind, I had a picture of the president appearing at his next press conference with one arm in a sling while he poked the air with the other, like he always did to emphasize a point. I thought about the experience I had just gone through with my cast and felt like the president and I would have something in common. Maybe he would even develop a good left-handed ping-pong game!

I returned to my exam.

A few minutes later the chimes on the P.A. system sounded again. Probably Mr. Pabst telling us what we already knew—that the president had been only slightly wounded and would be okay.

Mr. Pabst's voice initially cracked, and then he cleared his throat.

"Attention, all students and faculty. We have just received further word. President Kennedy died at Parkland Hospital in Dallas from a gunshot wound to the head."

I stared at the speaker centered above the American flag at the front of the classroom.

What!? I must be hearing things.

It felt like I was having another bad dream from which I hoped to wake.

The President—dead!?

No! It couldn't be!

There must have been some mistake.

C'mon, Mr. Pabst, tell us it was a mistake!

The President wasn't dead.

He couldn't be!

How?

Why?

My math teacher, usually a stoic man, stared at the speaker with the rest of us. In a hushed voice, he whispered, "My God!"

The rest of us looked around at each other and then back down at our test papers. Somehow this all-important exam had lost its significance. Who could possibly prove that triangles were congruent after what we had just heard?

Five minutes later a bell signaled the end of the period.

The trip back to homeroom, normally a happy event on a Friday afternoon, was subdued. Everyone seemed to be in a state of shock. On the bus ride home, I almost slugged a kid from my social studies class. He liked the Republicans and made a wise crack about how Barry Goldwater would now have a good chance of winning the next presidential election, which was a year away.

When I arrived home, I found my mother crying. I hugged her and then quickly turned on the television to get the news. The regularly scheduled programs on all the stations were preempted by ongoing news bulletins as Walter Cronkite, Chet Huntley, and David Brinkley provided up-to-date details. Lyndon Johnson had already been sworn in as the country's new president.

President Johnson.

It sounded odd at first and would take some time to get used to. Each station showed rerun after rerun of President Kennedy getting into his limousine at the Dallas airport, just as the motorcade began.

Now, he was dead.

It was too much to take in.

After supper, I headed directly to the block to discuss the latest events with the crowd. I spotted everyone sitting on Timmy's stoop. When I arrived, they were all talking about the assassination.

"They got the guy who did it," Pete reported.

"Yeah, his name is Oswald," Timmy added. "They say he also shot and killed a cop."

"I still can't believe it," I said. "At this time yesterday, the President was alive, maybe eating supper or reading the newspaper. Now he's dead. I can't deal with it."

"I'll tell you one thing," M.C. commented. "I'd hate to be this guy Oswald. No way is that guy going to live to stand trial. There must be a million people who'd love the honor of doing him in. I'd love to get my hands on him myself."

Then we all shared our memories of President Kennedy: his enthusiasm for the space program, his sense of humor, and how he stood up to the Russians during the Cuban Missile Crisis the year before.

I recalled staying up late on the night he defeated Richard Nixon during the 1960 presidential election, and how happy I felt when he won, as though my staying up late had contributed to his victory.

When the early editions of the next day's newspapers came out, we all scrutinized them for new details. Timmy bought editions of several papers, feeling that one day they would have historical value.

After we completed scanning the papers and talking about our memories of President Kennedy, there was nothing else to do, so we all went home.

The next couple of days were some of the longest in our lives. All the television stations kept reporting up-to-date details on the assassination and the funeral service. We were flooded with pictures of Lee Harvey Oswald, the Texas Book Depository, the mail-order murder weapon, and hundreds of other scenes. Periodically, there were flashbacks of happier times, like when Kennedy appeared with his children or cracked jokes about how he thought Vaughn Meader, a popular impersonator, sounded more like Kennedy's younger brother Teddy when imitating the president.

Now he was gone forever.

On Sunday, the twenty-fourth, after almost two days of

nonstop bulletins and flashbacks on television, I took a walk to the block to get some fresh air. I ran into some of the crowd, and since it was cold out, we decided to bypass the usual knitting mill hangout and head over to Bushwick gym. No one was in the mood for playing. We just sat on the bleachers talking about all the things that had happened in the past several days.

Eileen showed up eventually, and she'd brought Mary, a new friend from school who lived two blocks away. After we were all introduced, we went back to our conversations. A half hour later, M.C. appeared at the entrance to the gym. We called out to him, and he hurried over with an excited look on his face. Halfway to us, he blurted out, "They got him! They got Oswald!"

When he reached us, he filled us in on the details. "They got him," he repeated. "They got Oswald. They were transferring him to another jail, and some guy named Jack Ruby just walked up to him and shot him. It was all right there on the television!"

After all the trauma of the past few days, the news of Oswald's death came as no shock.

The president was dead, and now the guy who killed him was dead. There appeared to be nothing else to do.

We stayed talking on the bleachers for a long while and agreed to suspend all games on the block for a week, out of respect for the President we had loved. Then we all took a walk up to St. Brigid's to light some candles.

Up until that single act of violence in Dallas, our lives on the block had pretty much been insulated from the events of the outside world.

Now, suddenly, we felt caught up in an inexplicable and

violent storm that had penetrated our world and, along with it, our innocence.

There was nothing we could do except hang close together in the hopes of riding it out.

And that's exactly what we did.

Chapter XII

The Four Knights

Over the next month or so, we, along with the entire country, slowly tried to recover from the tragedy in Dallas. Towns and cities across the country made symbolic efforts to honor J.F.K. in one way or another. In New York City, Idlewild Airport was renamed John F. Kennedy International Airport. Cape Canaveral, the Florida site of the space program that Kennedy had so strongly supported, was also renamed in his honor.

The country struggled to return to normal and adjust to our new president, Lyndon Johnson. Though Johnson was considered highly qualified, his folksy southern style was a marked contrast to President Kennedy's youth and charisma.

For the crowd, it also felt like the emotional storm from November was finally passing, and our lives on the block returned to normal. Having regained the full use of my right wrist, I was now able to deal with school in a routine manner, and I welcomed the luxury of completing my homework and going to bed at a reasonable hour. For the others on the block, school had also become routine. On those rare school nights when we found time to get together, we headed to the recreation center, where a new game room had just opened. In contrast to the big noisy gym, the game room was a quieter, more intimate environment, where we could listen to records and play ping-pong or bumper pool.

In early January 1964, after Christmas vacation, we were all back to school and getting ready to take midterm exams. One night, while I was studying and my brother was shining the same pair of shoes for the fifth time, a radio announcer introduced a song called "I Want To Hold Your Hand" by a new British group called the Beatles.

When the song came on, we both stopped what we were doing to listen to it.

Though the lyrics were straightforward, the song had a catchy beat and a style that was different from that of the Four Seasons, the Beach Boys, and other popular American rock groups. When the song ended, my brother and I looked at each other and agreed that we liked the sound. When we turned on another station, we heard the song again. It felt like something special was happening.

A few weeks later, our initial feelings were validated. All the radio stations were not only playing "I Want To Hold Your Hand" but also several other songs by the Beatles, all of which seemed to be released one after the other. Their records got played nonstop, and pictures of the band members soon flooded television, newspapers, and popular magazines.

Almost overnight, John, Paul, George, and Ringo became household names, not only through their music but also in fashion trends, like their long moppy hairstyles, bell-bottom suits, and high black boots dubbed "Beatle Boots," which quickly appeared in the window of the local Tom McAn shoe store. Albums, posters, hairstyles, boots, buttons, and any other items associated with the Beatles sold like hotcakes. In early February, the Beatles arrived in the United States for their first American tour. They appeared at New York City's

Carnegie Hall and then on *The Ed Sullivan Show*. The night they appeared with Sullivan, frequent camera scans of the audience showed it packed with girls in their late teens and early twenties, all screaming and crying, "I love you!" as the band performed onstage. Sullivan, visibly pleased by the reactions of the audience, tried to maintain his cool after the last song, but he had to raise his voice to be heard above the screams and moans of the audience. Sullivan soon had even more reason to be pleased when his show's rating was the highest in its history. The Beatles were quickly invited back for a second appearance. In a relatively short time, not only did their music spread like wildfire but the Beatles became idols and role models for millions of kids, who let their hair grow and rushed off to buy Beatle Boots.

Even on the block, the Beatles made an impact. The Twins and Lisa all ran out to buy Beatles 45s and the first album, appropriately titled *Meet The Beatles*. Buttons proclaiming "I Love The Beatles" or "I Love Ringo" also became standard items in their daily apparel. On the other hand, the guys talked about how great it must be to tour the world and be on the Sullivan show. We soon discussed starting our own band. If the Beatles could become famous, why couldn't we?

M.C. kidded about how "I Love M.C." buttons would replace those with Ringo's name on them. Shortly afterward, I started guitar lessons at a music store next to the Ridgewood Theater on Myrtle Avenue. The store was run by a German couple, both in their mid-fifties. Up until the dawn of the Beatles, they'd gotten most of their business supplying instruments for St. Brigid's fife and drum corps or providing accordion lessons for Lawrence Welk fans.

Now it was a whole new ballgame.

Everybody and their sister wanted to learn how to play the guitar or drums.

"Forget 'Yankee Doodle Dandy,'" I told them when I signed up to take lessons. "How long will it take me to learn how to play like the Beatles?"

The German couple desperately tried to get up to speed with the changing environment and the increased demand for lessons.

Before my first lesson, the husband started giving me pointers on showbiz. "You got to have a gimmick," he began juicily. "I know what. We'll call you the Red Beatle!" His behaving like a German Ed Sullivan wasn't really cutting it for me. I felt like a young sports prospect getting playing tips from Howard Cosell, so I ignored the showbiz advice and eagerly looked forward to my first lesson with the actual teacher.

"This is the first string," the older Italian instructor began. "It's called the E string."

"Okay, okay, the E string. Now, when do we play 'I Want To Hold Your Hand'?"

"You will! You will! But first you need to be able to read the notes for each of the strings."

Wonderful. I'd have to learn the notes for *six* strings. At three dollars per lesson, I'd be eighteen dollars in the hole before I could even play a song.

Faithfully, I practiced my lessons, sometimes moving ahead to the next string to speed up the process. The Beatles were coming out with new songs at a rate of almost one per week, and all I had to show for my lessons was "Yankee Doodle Dandy"!

Around the time I started lessons, Timmy got his hands on

a secondhand set of drums from one of his brother's friends. The front of the bass drum was torn, but its rear skin still made a loud thumping sound. In combination with the snare drum, tom-tom, and full set of symbols, Timmy could already bang away to the beat of the latest songs.

Dissatisfied with the snail's pace of my teacher, I bought sheet music to the latest Beatles songs, and in between lessons, I attempted to learn the more complicated modern stuff. While I could play individual notes well, I had difficulty learning chords, which required holding down several strings at once.

I continued to nudge my instructor to go faster, and I guess he figured that if he didn't, I wasn't going to stick around too long.

"Okay, okay!" he relented. "I'll teach you how to play chords."

There was progress, but still not enough.

Timmy and I practiced in his basement. While he banged away, I tried in vain to keep up with the music. At home, I practiced in front of the same mirror where I had taught myself the mashed potato. Pete and M.C. asked us how things were coming along because our plan was to play music while M.C. and Pete took care of the singing and an easy-to-play tambourine. On weekends, we all got together in Timmy's basement and worked on the latest songs. We also worked on our act.

The first thing we did was cut out a piece of oak tag paper to cover the front opening of the bass drum. After that, we needed a name for our group. We tested out a few possibilities on the Twins and Lisa, and after careful deliberation, we settled on The Four Knights. M.C. designed a "4/K" monogram, which we printed on the bass drum using gold sparkles.

Now we were really rolling!

Initially, with my acoustic guitar, I got drowned out by the boom of Timmy's drums and the screeching of M.C. and Pete as they attempted to hit high notes. In no time at all, it was clear that I needed an electric guitar and amplifier. Timmy and I went window-shopping at the Myrtle Avenue music stores. While Timmy checked out the latest drums, I scanned a multitude of guitars that hung precariously along several walls.

Fender and Gretsch were the two most popular brands at the time. Unfortunately, they were expensive—very expensive. A Gretsch or Fender guitar and amplifier with the required echo-chamber effect cost two to three hundred dollars. No way my parents could afford that kind of bread, even if I got asked to join the Beatles.

As luck would have it, a few days after our shopping excursion, I received a copy of the latest catalog from Lafayette Electronics. I had worked on an electronics project in school and, having ordered parts from them, had been placed on their mailing list. I browsed through the catalog and, out of curiosity, turned to the index to see if they carried electric guitars. To my pleasant surprise, they did. I located the appropriate pages, and one guitar caught my eye. It was a slim brown solid-body guitar with a yellow starburst design in front, double pickups (two microphones), a vibrator bar for sound effects, and a fast-action neck with inlaid rosewood markers. After studying the description a few times, I glanced down at the price: "Special Sale $49.95."

Not bad, not bad at all! Along with the guitar, there was a good deal on a small amplifier and carrying case. The complete package, kit and caboodle, could be purchased for the bargain-basement price of $69.95!

Now the only problem I had was convincing my parents to shell out that kind of money.

That Saturday, while my mother was food shopping at the local A&P, I approached my father, who was home from work. I figured I would start slowly and then ease into the subject.

"Hi, Dad," I began. "How's work?"

"Okay, Son. How's school going?"

"Fine. I did really well on my midterms and should have a pretty good report card this period."

"Good! I'm glad to hear it. I'm proud of the way you're doing in school. I wish your brother's grades were as good as yours. Keep up the good work!"

"Thanks, Dad. I'll try."

Silence followed as my father went back to his newspaper and coffee. I continued sitting at the table with my head propped up by one arm, thinking about how to get the conversation started again.

Sports, I thought. *Let's try sports and see what happens.*

"Who do you like in the fight between Sonny Liston and Cassius Clay, Dad?"

"Liston," he responded matter-of-factly. "Clay does a lot of talking, but Liston is a hard puncher. I'll be surprised if it goes two rounds."

"Yeah, that's what I think too."

More silence.

Got to be more direct. No more beating around the bush.

"Dad, what would you say if I asked if I could get an

electric guitar?"

"Sounds to me like that's what you're doing now."

I smiled nervously. It seemed like the older I got, the smarter my father got.

"Yeah, I guess you could say that."

"What's wrong with the guitar you have now? That seems to be okay. You only just started taking lessons. Why not wait until you know how to play better?"

This was going to be as difficult as I thought it would be.

"Well, if I had an electric guitar, it would help me learn faster. With my current guitar, I have to press down hard on the strings in order to get a clear sound. With an electric guitar, it's a lot easier, and I could learn to play chords faster."

"An electric guitar costs a lot of money, doesn't it?"

I wasn't sure if he had bought the chord story or was looking for another reason to tell me no. Better to continue slowly. I took out the Lafayette catalog, which I just happened to have handy, and flipped to the page with the electric guitars on it.

"Not really. Here, I saw this electric guitar in this catalog. It only costs $49.95 and has two pickups and an echo bar. Look!"

My instincts told me to start out with the lower price. I turned my chair around to show my father. He put down his newspaper and glanced at the picture while he sipped his coffee.

"Forty-nine ninety-five, you say? That's nothing to sneeze at. What is this thing with it called an amplifier?"

So much for the go-slow strategy.

"Oh, that," I said nonchalantly. "That's the thing you plug the guitar into in order to make the sound come out."

"Is that included in the price?"

"Uh, no, Dad. That's extra."

I didn't have to go through the arithmetic. Even though my father drove trailer trucks down at the Brooklyn Navy Yard for a living, he was good at math. People in the family said he was the one that I got my math aptitude from.

"The guitar and amplifier come to $69.95," I said.

The tone of his reply seemed to go up at the same time his eyes did. "That is a lot of money."

Now I had to do some very fast talking.

"Well, Dad, it's really not a lot of money when you realize that most electric guitars and amplifiers cost over a hundred dollars, sometimes even two or three times that amount. I've never asked you for anything like this before, and I'm willing to pay for part of it."

Then I used the old guilt ploy about how my brother had gotten a lot of things I hadn't because he was older. This wasn't necessarily true, but I figured it couldn't hurt. I then reminded him that he had bought my brother a new bicycle that later got passed down to me, scratched and used.

I played another guilt card and reminded him that he and my mom, along with an aunt and uncle, had thrown a big party for my brother and my cousin Tommy when they received Holy Confirmation, while I'd only had a small party in our house.

After hearing enough of my guilt-inducing stories, my father looked like he might cave in.

Guilt… sickening to use, but effective.

So as not to leave my father with an unbearably heavy conscience, I offered to pay for the amplifier and the case.

My efforts were successful. A week later my father,

brother, and I took a trip to a nearby Lafayette Electronics store to look at the guitar. My brother had just gotten his learner's permit, so my father let him drive while I sat in the back of our 1951 Dodge, praying that we would make it to the store in one piece.

Rather than wait the ten minutes it took for my brother to park the car in a space big enough for a city bus, I rushed ahead to the store. Once inside, I headed straight for the musical instruments. The guitar I had spotted in the catalog was out front, gleaming in the sunlight that beamed through the store's front window. A short while later, my father and brother arrived. My father was visibly annoyed at how long it had taken my brother to park. *Just my luck. I finally get my father all the way here and my brother blows it for me by getting him ticked off.* My father was slow to anger, but once he got there, look out! My mother was the parental disciplinarian, usually with the aid of a strap, but my father was the one we feared most, even though he never laid a hand on us.

Hoping to change my father's mood, I called out to him. "Here it is, Dad, over here! Isn't it a beauty?"

My father carefully inspected the guitar.

Spotting a prospective buyer, a large balding salesman headed in our direction. "Hi! Can I help you with something?"

"You sure can!" I said. "I'd like to try out this electric guitar to see how it sounds."

"Sure. No problem!"

In a matter of minutes, I was hooked up to a large amplifier. I tuned the guitar and strummed the few chords I knew to give my father the impression that I knew what I was doing. Hearing the sound of the guitar, other customers looked over with interest, and a small crowd gathered around. I suddenly became deathly afraid of embarrassing myself in front of them and my father.

Once I felt certain the strings were tuned, I headed into three songs I knew well: "Pipeline," "Walk, Don't Run," and finally, "I Want To Hold Your Hand."

Though I tried hard not to screw up, I did make a few mistakes. All the same, I felt I had made a respectable showing for myself, and when I finished the last song, I got scattered applause from the onlookers.

My brother patted me on the back and said, "All right! My little brother, the rock star!"

My father smiled and asked the salesman if the guitar had volume controls on it. When the salesman responded that it did, my father seemed relieved. He agreed to buy it along with the smaller amplifier.

I clutched the guitar in its case, and my brother carried the small amplifier out to the car. Not even my brother driving home could diminish my joy as I sat in the back seat glowing, dreaming of the day when The Four Knights might appear on *The Ed Sullivan Show*.

Later that night I called Timmy and gave him the good news about my instrument. In no time flat, he, M.C., and Pete arrived at my house to help lug the guitar and amplifier to our basement "studio," where, despite Timmy's mother's demands to play quietly, we blasted away.

"Look out, Beatles!" we cried. "Here come The Four Knights!"

Chapter XIII

The Case of Rupert Knickerbocker

Despite many lengthy and noisy practice sessions down Timmy's cellar, it didn't take long for us to realize that The Four Knights were not going to make it to the Sullivan show. While we no longer continued as a music group, the experience did bring the four of us closer as friends, and we maintained a one-for-all, all-for-one relationship afterward.

Later that winter a serious problem developed on the block involving Pete's younger brother, Stephen. One crisp Sunday afternoon, Stephen came home crying and telling Pete he had been bullied by a much bigger and older kid who did not live on the block. The bully was visiting a house up near Ridgewood Place. Pete was babysitting that day and couldn't come out, but through his bedroom window, he briefed M.C., Timmy, and me on the situation as the girls looked on with concerned expressions.

"All I know," Pete said, "is that Stephen came home crying about how some kid he had never seen before took his football. I don't know who this kid is or why he took the ball, but I want you guys to do some detective work and get it back!"

As Pete talked, we asked questions and tried to gather evidence the way we had seen Sergeant Joe Friday do countless times on *Dragnet*. When we were satisfied that we had all the information, we hopped off the stoop and headed up the block to the scene of the crime.

"A strange older kid," M.C. recounted. "Let's find out if there's anyone around who fits that description."

We talked to a few kids with whom Stephen had been playing when his football was taken. They told us that the perpetrator had come from a house two doors from the corner.

We glanced at the house in question. The entire area was deserted. It was still relatively early in the day, so we set up a stakeout across the street in the knitting mill doorway. Timmy then went to get hot chocolates while M.C. and I kept our eyes peeled.

At around 3:00 p.m., a tall kid fitting the suspect's description emerged from the house we were staking out.

He was alone.

Rather than wait for Timmy to return, M.C. and I headed over to ask a few questions. From the looks of the guy, he was older, perhaps fifteen, and taller than us by about three inches.

"Hey, fella," M.C. called out as we approached, "can we talk to you for a minute?"

The kid froze in his tracks and put his hands inside the pockets of his winter coat.

When we got closer, I took over the questioning. "Say, you wouldn't have seen a football that belongs to one of the smaller kids down the block?"

It was cold out and I didn't feel like beating around the bush.

"And what if I did?" the kid shot back in a voice dripping with trouble.

"The kid happens to be my kid brother," I said, role-playing a bit. "And I think you ought to go get the ball if you know where it is."

The kid didn't say anything but pulled out a beer bottle from his coat pocket and smashed it against a nearby cast-iron fence.

"You want it so badly, why don't you come get it? If you're lucky, maybe I'll only get you in the face with this!"

He jabbed the broken bottle toward us, and we quickly stepped back. The jagged edges of glass glistened with danger. We needed to play it cool.

"Hey, listen," M.C. said, his voice taking on a more conciliatory tone. "All we want is the kid's football. He's only eight years old. What's the big deal?"

"Well, if you want the ball, come and get it," the kid challenged again, keeping the broken bottle out in the open. Then he picked up the lid of a garbage pail. There, on top, sat Stephen's small powder-blue football.

The sight of it made me angry.

"Hey, you big punk," I yelled. "Do you get your thrills taking away toys from little kids? Why don't you pick on someone your own size?"

"Well, well," the kid said, "who do we have here? John Wayne? If you're so brave, why don't you just come and take the ball away?"

"Why don't you put down the bottle, and we'll talk it over?" M.C. said.

We both knew that if the kid put down the bottle, he was in for trouble.

The kid also knew it.

He held onto the bottle and walked toward us again.

At that moment, Timmy returned with the hot chocolates

and spotted us.

"Hey, what's happening?" he yelled as he approached.

When the kid saw Timmy, he quickly realized the new three-against-one odds and backed off.

"Timmy," M.C. said, "let me introduce you. This here is the thug who gets his thrills stealing footballs from little kids. When he's not stealing toys, he likes to play Marlon Brando with a broken bottle."

I glanced at Timmy, whose eyes quickly focused on the bottle.

"You guys think you're so tough, three against one. If you want trouble, I got it right here. Who wants to be the first one to lose an eye?"

"Get a grip on yourself," Timmy said.

At that moment, a loud voice called out from the doorway of the house the kid was visiting. When he heard his name, he backed up and discreetly dropped the bottle by a parked car.

Once he was inside the house, we retrieved Stephen's football from the garbage pail. Then we headed back to Pete's house to return the ball and plan our next steps.

When we gave Pete the ball, we filled him in.

"He *what*?" Pete asked when he heard the business about the broken bottle and the bully's offer to perform free plastic surgery on us. "This kid sounds as though he's not all there."

"Not all there?" M.C. said. "This kid ain't there at all!"

"He's so far off the wall," Timmy said, "that he makes M.C. seem normal!"

That comment prompted some snickering.

"Okay, okay, let's settle down here, girls," I said, trying to get the discussion back on track. "Whatta we gonna do now?"

"What can we do?" M.C. asked. "We got the football back;

why look for more trouble? Maybe the kid won't be out again anyway."

"Let's take a walk up the block again and hang out," Timmy suggested. "If he comes out, we'll deal with him. If he doesn't, then we won't."

We nodded in agreement.

"Let me know how you guys make out," Pete said as we left. Just before he got inside, little Stephen poked his head through the open door and thanked us for getting his ball back.

Once outside the kid's house, we headed back to our stakeout spot. Despite two rounds of hot chocolate, the cold weather penetrated our bodies. Our faces went numb and our feet froze, so we hopped up and down, trying to keep warm.

At 6:00 p.m., we called it a night and decided to head home. It was getting dark and the thought of thawing out in a nice warm house was too much to pass up.

As luck would have it, just as we were about to leave, the kid came out of the house. But when he spotted us, he ducked back inside.

We waited.

A minute later, he reappeared, this time accompanied by two older men. We saw him point to us and say something to the men. They stepped off their stoop and headed in our direction. Suddenly, we were on the defensive.

"Hey, you!" one of the men shouted.

We looked around, not entirely sure he was talking to us. Unfortunately, he was.

"You three," he said. "Why don't you leave my son alone? Don't you kids having anything better to do than gang up on somebody, three against one?"

The two men and the kid had now crossed the street and

were only six feet away from us.

"You wanna explain what you're talking about?" M.C. snapped back.

"You know exactly what I'm talking about," the other guy said. Meanwhile, the kid stood there with a big smirk on his face.

"I don't think you really know what's going on," I said, trying to sound polite yet firm. "If you're talking about the unfair odds, ask your son why he took a rubber football away from an eight-year-old kid!"

"That's a lie! I didn't take anyone's football."

"Yes, you did!" Timmy countered. "You even showed us where you hid it in the garbage pail."

"Which garbage pail?" the father asked.

"That one over there," I said, pointing.

The kid's father went over to the pail and removed the lid. The ball wasn't there, of course.

"I don't see any ball in here."

Rather than give us a chance to explain, the kid used the missing ball as an opportunity to make up another lie. "You three guys asked me for money, and when I said I wouldn't give it to you, you threatened me."

"Where do you guys live?" the father asked.

"Those two live down the block," the uncle said, pointing to M.C. and Timmy. "I don't know where this kid lives." He pointed to me.

"I've got a good mind to go down to your houses and talk to your parents!" the father said. "It's a shame that a decent kid can't come and visit relatives on this block without being bullied by local punks like you three!"

The situation was getting totally out of hand. Not only was

the kid getting off scot-free, but it looked like we were going to take the heat for something we didn't even do.

"Hey, hold on a minute!" M.C. said.

"Who are you calling punks?" Timmy said.

Both the kid's father and uncle had the smell of beer on their breath, and it looked like they might try to take matters into their own hands.

"I'm calling you three punks," the father said. "It's three against three now. How come you punks aren't acting so tough?"

Yeah, it was three against three, all right. Two grown men and a fifteen-year-old kid against two fourteen-year-olds and a thirteen-year-old. We had as much of a chance against them as a submarine with a screen door.

Better to keep talking, I thought.

"Listen," I yelled, directing my attention toward the kid. "Are you claiming that you didn't take the football and then threaten us with a broken bottle?"

The kid laughed. "Oh, that's even better!" He shrugged his shoulders. "First you accuse me of taking some kid's football, and now you're saying I threatened you with a broken bottle. You guys can really make up some wild lies!"

"C'mon," M.C. said, "you stood almost in the exact spot where you are now and threatened to slash our faces if we tried to get the football back."

"Hold on there a minute! Are you saying that my son threatened you with a broken bottle? That's absurd!"

"It's the truth!" Timmy pleaded. "Your son told us that if we wanted the ball back, we'd have to go through him—and he was holding a broken bottle in his hand when he said it."

"And I suppose the mysterious bottle is in the pail where

the ball was supposed to have been?" the uncle asked sarcastically.

"No!" I shot back. "As a matter of fact, he threw it under one of the cars parked in front of your house. The brown Rambler over there!"

"I did not!" the kid said.

"Well, there's only one way to find out," Timmy said. "Let's go check."

M.C. scurried over to the Rambler and slid underneath, as he had done hundreds of times during stickball games. This time he was particularly careful because of the shattered fragments from the bottle. Gently, he dragged out some of the larger pieces, using his foot.

"Here's the evidence! Exhibit A!" M.C. exclaimed, as he presented the pieces to the father.

"For all I know," the kid screamed, "you could have planted that bottle under the car yourselves! You can't prove I had that bottle."

It was sickening how the kid continued to deny ever having seen the bottle that was right in front of him. Had this been *Dragnet*, Sergeant Joe Friday would have sent the evidence to the lab to check for fingerprints. Unfortunately, it was not that simple for us.

"Ha so," Timmy said in his Charlie Chan voice. "Let me ask you this." He turned his attention to the uncle. "Are you drinking Rupert Knickerbocker beer inside your house right now?"

The two men looked at each other with surprised expressions.

"As a matter of fact, we are drinking Rupert Knickerbocker!" the father answered, his voice taking on a softer tone.

"Well, that's the same brand as the label on the broken bottle right here!" Sensing that the tide was turning in our favor, Timmy continued. "How did this broken bottle of Rupert Knickerbocker beer get out here, underneath this car, if your son didn't bring it outside?"

"That's a good question," the father responded as he turned to his son with an expression of shock and surprise. "Did you bring that beer out here? I told you I would let you have some inside."

"Bu-bu-but dad," the kid said, "I didn't. They're lying!"

The gig was up, but the kid refused to face up to it.

Without another word, the father gave the kid a slap right across his face. "Don't lie to me! Get inside the house. Now! I'll take care of you later."

As the kid retreated into the house crying, we stood there feeling vindicated.

"Listen, fellas," the father said, "I'm really sorry about all of this."

"That's okay," we muttered, not knowing what else to say.

"No, no," the father said. "Here's a few bucks. Why don't you kids go get yourselves something hot to drink? You must be frozen."

He took out three one-dollar bills and extended them in our direction.

We looked at the money but decided that we didn't want to be bought off. Stephen had his ball back, the kid had gotten what he deserved, and we were vindicated. That was enough.

"Nah, that's okay," we all said in one form or another.

"Are you sure?" the father asked again.

"Yeah," I said. "Anyway, it's getting late and we gotta

head home."

In one last apologetic act, the two men shook hands with each of us and told us what fine boys we were.

After the handshaking ceremony, we headed back to Pete's house, slapping each other five along the way.

"Way to go!"

"What detective work!"

"Joe Friday couldn't have done better!"

"You guys can thank me for getting the bottle!" M.C. said.

"Whaddaya mean—thank you?" Timmy asked indignantly. "I was the one who thought of the label!"

"Hey, hold on here," I said. "I was the one who spotted where the kid threw the bottle!"

We stopped in our tracks, looked at each other, and laughed.

"Never mind!" we all agreed.

Due to our collective detective efforts, we had successfully "smashed" The Case of Rupert Knickerbocker!

Chapter XIV

The Journey to O.Z.

When spring rolled around, the Mets moved into the newly completed Shea Stadium in Flushing, Queens. Back in the neighborhood, we Bombers and the Palmetto Street Royals joined forces to try our luck down at Bushwick's newly renovated softball field.

Several years prior, when my brother and I were younger, we used to watch my father play softball there on a team sponsored by Connell's Bar and Grill, where my father was a regular patron. The old field was the neighborhood's equivalent of Yankee Stadium. The only word to describe it was HUGE, and whenever I went there to watch my father play, I was overwhelmed by its size. The left-field fence looked like it was a mile away from home plate, and the only person I ever saw hit a ball over it was a big Italian guy named Sal, who played center field for Connell's. In addition to its size, the old field was a real adventure for infielders because the concrete surface had more cracks and craters than the moon. On more than one occasion, I saw easy ground balls take bad hops over the heads of startled infielders.

By the time our crowd used the field, it had undergone major renovations. Part of the old left-field area was now the site of Bushwick's new indoor pool and game room. New twenty-foot-high chain-link perimeter fences had been installed, and the playing field was smoothly blacktopped. Along the fences, basketball hoops and backboards had been hung fifteen feet apart. To compensate for the shorter distance to the left-field fence, the new home run boundary had been extended thirty feet to the right of the left-field foul line. Though a little shorter than the old park, the new home run boundary still required a long hit to clear it.

With our teams combined, the Bombers and the Royals barely had enough players for a nine-man softball team, even if everyone showed up. When we were short a man or two, we'd pick up players who were hanging around the field, looking to get into a game. The field was located at the crossroads of a community in transition. To the south, the neighborhood was primarily Puerto Rican with a few pockets of Italians. Eastward, the area was primarily Black, and the west side was a tapestry of Puerto Ricans, Italians, and Germans. Finally, north of the field, where our block was located, the neighborhood was mostly Italian, bordered by a heavy German area farther north in Glendale.

The field, like Bushwick's gym, was a peaceful, friendly gathering place for all these nationalities. During the week, the action was sporadic. Usually there were enough guys around to play one, maybe two, seven-inning games of underhand fast pitch. On weekends, however, the action picked up, and in addition to the teams playing on the field, there'd be several others waiting to challenge the winner. Many of the weekend players were older—not necessarily better, but older. Some of the players brought coolers of beer and soda, while others brought wives and kids, making it a family outing. The games were often played for money, mostly a dollar or two a man, sometimes more if there were side bets. The first couple of times we went down to the field, we were able to hold our own with the local competition. Our infield was good, but our outfield was weak. Timmy played first base, I played second, Pete was at shortstop, and Davey from the Royals was at third. Hank, the former handball champ from Palmetto Street, was the catcher, and a kid named Ricky, one of the younger members of the Palmetto crowd, pitched. In the outfield, M.C. played left field, and—if they showed up—Richie Soo played right field while the big German kid, George, played center.

Unfortunately, Richie often had to work at his parents' restaurant, and George was busy dating a girl from a distant neighborhood. Most of the time, this meant we had to pick up outfielders from amongst local players, who were generally not good and who made catching every fly ball an adventure.

Toward the second week in July, it became apparent that we needed to solidify certain positions to become competitive. The outfield and pitching positions were particularly weak. While Ricky did his best to keep the ball over the plate and not walk too many batters, his pitches got hit a lot. The ground balls to the infield usually were handled without a problem, but our outfield killed us as routine fly balls frequently turned into unnecessary home runs. The unfortunate results were that we paid out more money than we took in and had to wait long periods before we could play again after a loss. It was definitely not our idea of a fun way to spend a Sunday.

One team we played against was the Squires. Most of the Squires also lived on Woodbine Street but two blocks farther south, down near Central Avenue. They found themselves in a similar situation to ours. They too rarely had enough guys for a full team, and their fielding problems were the reverse of ours. Their outfielders and catcher were good, but their infield was weak. The Squires fully reflected the ethnic cross section of their neighborhood. Their catcher and third baseman, Bo and Joe, respectively, were both Italian. Their shortstop, Pastor, and their two outfielders, Gary and George, aka "the G brothers," were all Puerto Rican, and their pitcher was an Irish kid named Eddy.

One day as the Squires and our team waited on the sidelines, we started talking and realized the mutual benefits of merging teams. This move, however, did not come without problems since it meant that players on both teams would have to change positions or ride the bench. On our team, the players most affected by the potential merger were M.C., Ricky, and me.

In the outfield, the G brothers were by far the best at their positions. George had lightning speed covering left field, and Gary's rocket-like throwing arm made him an ideal choice for center field. The right-field position, however, was another story, though there weren't too many lefties who could pull the ball down the right-field line. Plus, there were real problems when they did hit it there because when the field had been blacktopped, the right-field area had been sloped downward to help with drainage problems. The result was that it felt like you were throwing uphill, and M.C. had neither good speed nor a strong throwing arm—weaknesses often capitalized on by opposing teams.

In the infield, the situation was more complex. Joe, the third baseman for the Squires, had a rifle arm, an important asset for playing that position. At shortstop, it was a toss-up between our Davey and their Pastor, with preferences split along team loyalties. Since Davey and Pastor were both excellent hitters, it was important to keep them both in the lineup, so we compromised by having Pastor stay at short and moving Davey to second base. It worked out well, and they soon became the best double-play combination in the neighborhood.

Having been displaced from his old position, Pete moved to right field. Over at first base, Timmy held on to his original position, at least initially. He had a large first baseman's glove, similar to one used by his idol, Joe Pepitone, of the Yankees. Most of the time, he scooped up every ball that came his way. Sometimes, however, he had problems handling throws from Joe, who had a strong arm but could throw a little wild. When it came to hitting, Timmy was also okay but had problems handling fast underhand pitching. For me, the choices boiled down to sitting on the bench as a pinch hitter or trying my hand at pitching. With the merger of the two teams, the pecking order of our standing in the larger group also changed. We were no longer just members of the block. Now we had to earn our way onto the team. I wasn't crazy about the situation, but I had limited options.

When the teams first merged, we had two captains. Pete represented the Bomber Royal contingent and Joe the Squires. To the chagrin of some of us, it appeared that deals were being made without our input. For example, Joe and Pete had made the decision to look for another first baseman and pitcher. Some of the old Bombers and Royals felt that the problem wasn't with Timmy but with Joe's erratic throwing arm. The members of the Squires disagreed, and since Joe was a co-captain of the team, he pressed the issue.

Due to the changes from the merger and the growing criticism of his skills, Timmy lost interest in playing and started spending more time by himself, training his dog and practicing the drums. Meanwhile, Pete and Joe lined up a potential replacement: a tall Black guy name Tommy, whom we knew from the night center. Tommy's size became a major asset in reaching wild throws from Joe that would have sailed over Timmy's head.

The other position being actively scouted was pitcher, which didn't sit too well with me because it looked like that was my only hope of starting. Playing ball and hanging out with the crowd were especially important to me, so I stuck it out. But I was hurt that Pete seemed anxious to recruit a left-handed pitcher he'd only seen play a few times. Though Pete didn't know the guy's actual name, he referred to him as "Pepitone" because he looked like a small young version of Joe Pepitone.

One night, on our way to a practice game, I was walking up the brick steps that led to the field when I heard some commotion. When I reached the top of the steps, I saw what all the excitement was about. The new kid, Pepitone, was throwing warm-up pitches on the sidelines, and several players were standing around watching every pitch he threw. Pete was right beside him, acting like his agent. I felt hurt but strolled over to get a look for myself. Every time Pepitone threw a strike, Pete called out, "Way to go!" or "That's the one!"

The words pierced like daggers.

Rather than throw in the towel, I decided to make my stand on the pitcher's mound. If I lost out to Pepitone, it would be because he was better, not because someone *thought* he was better.

During the game later that evening, Pepitone pitched. He had good control but not a lot of speed. His best pitch was a wide arcing curveball that seemed to bend a foot and a half.

I studied his curveball and later practiced throwing it with Bo. To my pleasant surprise, I received a lot of support from the Squires, particularly Joe and Bo. Bo caught for me and said that I threw the ball much harder than Pepitone and that I just needed to work on my control. Joe liked the idea of having a pitcher who could throw hard, and he seemed to identify with my control problems. Joe also confided that he wasn't as confident about Pepitone as Pete was, and he felt I might win the pitching role with work.

When I practiced with Bo on the sidelines, I found myself throwing very hard. Occasionally, I got wild, and the pitches sailed over his head or bounced on the ground, prompting him to trot out and say, "I'm gonna kick your ass if you keep throwing that way."

I knew he was only mad because he wanted me to pitch well, and after a while, "kick your ass" became an inside code between us whenever my control was off.

The situation with Pepitone continued for another week, and except for pitching, it looked like the rest of the team was beginning to jell.

Based on our progress, Joe booked a game with a team from Ozone Park, Queens, otherwise known as O.Z. One of Joe's cousins lived in O.Z., and whenever he visited, he got challenged by his cousin's friends about scheduling a softball game for "big money." When the game was finally arranged, the guys from O.Z. told Joe that they would cover whatever amount we wanted to bet.

In preparation for the big game, we played every day and again at night. When it came to selecting the starting pitcher, some of the guys wanted Pepitone and others wanted me.

Oddly enough, it was fate that made the final decision. A day or two before the big game, Pepitone went to Pete and Joe and told them he couldn't make the big game.

"Maybe we can get the game postponed or rescheduled," he suggested.

Pete and Joe stepped aside to discuss the matter, and Joe reacted loudly enough for me to overhear. "What's he—some kind of prima donna? The game is scheduled, and we can't back out. I don't like his attitude, anyway."

After further discussion, Joe went over to Bo and spoke with him. They were too far away for me to hear, but Bo nodded his head a few times in agreement. At the conclusion of their conversation, Bo headed in my direction. "Hey, D," he said, "kick your ass! Get a ball and start warming up. Pepitone can't make the game at O.Z. You're pitching. It's your game to win or lose!"

A minute later Joe came over. "Hey, Danny," he said in his thick Brooklyn accent, "when we go to O.Z., you're pitching. I just want you to do me one favor and that's to try your best."

"I will," I replied, trying to suppress the smile on my face.

"Just between you and me, I wanted you to start anyway, even if Pepitone could make it."

"Thanks a lot, Joe. I won't let the guys or you down."

Afterward, I warmed up with Bo while the other guys practiced their hitting and fielding—and periodically glanced over to see how I was doing. I tried a couple of different deliveries to keep the ball low. After a few, I found a style that seemed to work well, and when I did it correctly, the ball stayed low and rose into the strike zone with good velocity. I also found that if I turned my wrist as I released the pitch— something I'd seen Pepitone do when he threw his curve—the ball would curve a lot. I made mental notes on what I was doing, and after a while, the ball was snapping into Bo's glove.

"Kick your ass!" Bo yelled with every strike.

Pete eventually wandered over. "Hey, Dan, how's it going?"

"Okay," I said, still annoyed by the way he had advocated so strongly for Pepitone.

"Well, get out there and give it your best."

"That's all I can do," I said coolly, figuring he'd get the message.

Pete went for more batting practice, and I continued throwing.

The night of the big game finally arrived. The field at O.Z. had lights, so there was no concern about the game being called because of darkness. Our entire team traveled there in a 1958 Oldsmobile convertible owned by an older guy, Eddie, who rented an apartment with his wife, Mitzi, in the three-family house that Pastor's family owned. Traveling to O.Z., we were a cramped, jumbled mass of multicolored arms and legs. Pete and I got stuck lying on the floor in the back, but we didn't mind since it helped keep Eddie from getting a ticket. It was quite the sight as a ragtag mix of Black, White, and Puerto Rican kids made their way into O.Z., which at the time was a heartland of blue-collar White America.

Upon arriving, we untangled ourselves and filed out of Eddie's car. Pete and I looked like a couple of rag dolls as we scraped ourselves off the floor. Once on the field, we snapped into our respective roles and got ready. Tommy unloaded and carried an old duffel bag filled with our bats and balls. Joe carried the gloves and Bo the catcher's mask. The rest of us scanned the playing field for areas that looked advantageous on offense or possibly troublesome on defense. I studied the fences to see how far back they went. Unfortunately, they weren't as far as I would have liked. The left-field fence was about as deep as the one in our home field except that it wasn't as high. Right field was L-shaped with a short fence, but the center-field area went far back. While I was relieved to learn that anything over the right-field fence was only a double, it was still something I had to be careful about. The main problem in center was the amount of ground that had to be covered. Since the right fielder was blocked by the short fence, the center fielder had to cover much more ground than usual. In view of this situation, we made several last-minute defensive adjustments. Gary, who was slower, was moved to left field. Tommy was shifted to center field and George was moved to right. In the infield, Pastor moved from shortstop to first base, Davey from second to short, and Pete from right field to second. Though the changes were significant, we felt comfortable making them since everyone had often played these positions in practice.

After settling into our dugout, we met the opposing team. They represented their neighborhood well. All were White blue-collar types who looked older than us because they already seemed to be shaving. Pete and Joe met the captain and co-captain and went over the ground rules. Then Bo collected the bets from our team, and true to their word, the guys from O.Z. covered all our money. Some of our players wagered large amounts—five or ten dollars each. Others, like me, went for a couple of bucks. Joe and Bo went for ten bucks each. During the meeting, one of the guys from O.Z. tried to be a smart-ass and offered to cover even more bets. Tommy took him up on his offer and held out a crisp twenty-dollar bill. The guy from O.Z. appeared surprised and, after a couple of deep swallows, dug into his jeans and came up with enough to match Tommy's bet.

When all the bets were finalized, the next step was to choose an umpire. We agreed with the choice of Eddy for calling balls and strikes, and one of the guys from O.Z. to umpire the bases. Each of the teams then took a turn practicing fielding and hitting.

As our team warmed up, I thought about the money riding on the game, which totaled close to a hundred dollars. Part of me felt pressured by the large amount, while another part of me felt that it was a vote of confidence from my teammates. Joe and Bo came over and uncharacteristically started kidding around to help lighten things up.

"Hey, Danny," Joe said, "I want you to go out there and pitch your best. I have ten bucks riding on this game, and if we lose, you're walking home. Got it?"

"Hey! Kick your ass, Joe!" Bo said. "Get away from my pitcher when he's warming up."

I laughed.

Then Pete stopped by. "Hey, how's it going?" he asked.

"Okay. I'm ready."

"Listen, Dan, I'm sorry about the stuff with Pepitone. I should have handled it better."

"No problem. It happens."

"Well, good luck out there."

After that, he went to take some batting practice, and I felt better. At least he had realized he was wrong. There was no sense holding any grudges, particularly now. I had a big game to pitch.

When the team from O.Z. took batting practice, I checked out their hitters. They had two, maybe three guys who looked like they might be trouble. I made mental notes on them. They also had a tall skinny guy nicknamed Bones, who held the bat with an unconventional cross-handed grip that resulted in him hitting to the opposite field a lot. Another thing to note, I thought.

Finally, it was time to begin. Joe and Pete met with the opposing captain and co-captain to flip a coin to determine which team would bat first. We won the toss and elected to bat last. Then our team ran out to take the field, and I walked to the pitcher's mound just like I had watched major league pitchers do on TV.

Eddy unwrapped a new Clincher softball from its box and tossed it to me. Another new ball would come into the game at the halfway mark.

During my warm-ups, I concentrated on starting low and getting my body behind my pitches like I had practiced with Bo. Usually, I could tell how I would do in a game based on the way I felt when I was warming up. Tonight, it was tough, however, because I felt tight. When two of my warm-up pitches sailed over Bo's head, some of the guys from O.Z. took note and got on me.

"Hey, guys, Red's throwing sky balls!"

Red. I hated that name. My father had red hair, and everyone called him Red. That was okay for him, but I didn't like it!

Joe trotted over from his third-base position.

"Just concentrate on what you're doing," he instructed. "Don't pay any attention to those guys. If they think they can get to you, they'll do it even more. Good luck!"

He went back to his position as I finished my warm-up.

"Batter up!" Eddy called out.

The chanting on both sides was loud and enthusiastic.

"Okay, Danny, let 'em have it!"

"LET'S DO IT TO THESE BUMS!" Tommy yelled from center field.

I carefully took the ball in my hands and juggled it until I held the stitching the way I liked it. I went into my motion and let the first pitch go.

"Outside!" Eddy yelled. "Ball one!"

The chatter behind me continued. "Okay, Danny, let's go, no sweat, mow 'em down!"

I wound up again and released the next pitch.

"High and inside! Ball two!"

The pitch had really taken off.

"Hey, D," Bo yelled, "just bring it down!"

After a few minor adjustments, the next pitch was on its way.

"Low! Ball three!"

Just missed again, dammit!

The O.Z. bench went wild.

"Hey, rag-arm!" they screamed. "You're gonna walk him—way to go!"

The guy at bat had hit one over the fence during practice. However, with a count of three balls and no strikes, I figured he'd be looking for a walk and would not swing at the next pitch. I went into my motion, but rather than throw hard, I lobbed the pitch over, hoping to get my first strike.

I guessed wrong.

The batter took a full swing and smashed the pitch clear over the left-field fence for a home run. As he rounded the bases, he grinned ear to ear and yelled to his teammates. "These guys are going to be a piece of cake!"

Joe looked like he was going to knock the runner out when he rounded third base. Instead, he just bit his glove in anger and frustration.

When the player reached home plate and turned to his dugout, the guys from O.Z. slapped him five. They looked noticeably confident, as though the game were already in the bag.

Bo came bouncing out to the pitcher's mound. "Don't let it get to you. These guys are a bunch of turkeys. Just keep throwing hard and get into your groove!"

He was right. I had played it safe and gotten smacked for a home run.

"Just let it go!" I muttered to myself. "If it's a strike, it's a strike! If it's not, it's not! If you're gonna go down, then go down fighting!"

Had this been a Popeye cartoon, it would have been the perfect time for me to take out my can of spinach and become a superman. Unfortunately, I had no spinach. Fortunately, the next batter up was Bones.

I reached back and let the ball loose. The pitch started out low, rose, and curved perfectly into the strike zone.

"Strike one!" Eddy bellowed.

The next pitch went the same way, and by the time Bones swung at it, the ball was already in Bo's glove.

"Strike two!" Eddy cried again.

The guys behind me came back to life.

"Way to go!"

"That's it!"

I tried a roundhouse curve next, and the ball broke so much

that Bones initially backed away, fearing it might hit him.

"Strike three, you're out!" Eddy roared.

Bones protested the call, but a teammate standing near home plate told him that the pitch had curved over the plate.

Now it felt like a whole new ball game!

The first two pitches to the next batter were also strikes.

With each strike, my confidence grew. I relaxed mentally and got into a good pitching groove. The last batter of the inning popped out to second base in a futile attempt just to hit the ball.

Now it was our turn at bat.

Even though we were down by a run, the way I'd pitched after the home run had seemed to pick the team up.

Pete, our first batter, drilled a ground ball up the middle on his first pitch. Our team let out a big roar.

Man on first.

Davey, our second hitter, lined the next pitch into the hole in right center. His legs moved like wheels, spinning around the bases. By the time the outfielder got to the ball, Dave was rounding second and heading for third. Bo, coaching third, signaled for to him to stop once he reached it. There was no sense in taking chances since we had already gotten the run back, and Davey was in great scoring position with no one out.

Our next batter was Joe, who lined a deep shot to left center field. Though their center fielder made a nice catch, the ball was deep enough for Davey to tag up from third and score easily. We had taken the lead. Our dugout was euphoric!

Bones, the O.Z. catcher, called time and walked out to talk to his pitcher. Now it was our turn to badger and brag.

"Hey, rag-arm, how's it feel now?" Pete screamed.

"It ain't over yet!" their pitcher yelled.

This was a good sign. If you got the opposing pitcher to yell from the field, it meant you were getting to him.

The next batter was Tommy, our cleanup hitter.

The first pitch came in low and rose just over his knees. On anyone else the pitch would have been a ball, high. But for Tommy it was a strike. He nodded his head and got set for the next pitch.

It approached him in an identical location, except this time Tommy was there to greet it with his bat. As fast as the ball came in, that's how fast it sailed out, up, and over the left-field fence.

A home run!

As Tommy trotted around the bases, the rest of us went bananas. I hadn't been this excited since the Dodgers–Yankees World Series.

Bones called time and consulted with his pitcher again.

It was beautiful!

O.Z. decided to leave their pitcher in the game. Our next two batters made out, but both had hit the ball extremely hard.

In the next inning, I picked up where I had left off, and every pitch I threw was a strike. The guys from O.Z. swung at everything, and I retired their side in only seven pitches.

When the guys from O.Z. returned to the field, they appeared shaken. We continued to hammer away at their pitcher, both verbally and with our bats, as we scored three more runs in the second inning and another three in the third. By the time we brought in the new ball midgame, we were winning 10–1!

In the fourth inning, I faced the guy who had hit the initial home run. I threw the ball as hard as I could, and it went high for ball one. I wanted to get this guy badly—very badly. Bo sensed I was pressing too much and gave me his famous, "Kick your ass!"

I got the message and settled down. The next pitch was the roundhouse curve ball. He popped it up right in front of me. Normally, a pitcher gets out of the way and lets one of the other fielders catch pop flies, but I wanted to make the play and get this guy out myself. "I got it, I got it, I got it!" I screamed at the top of my lungs. The other players quickly got the message and stayed clear.

When the ball snapped into my glove, I squeezed it with a sense of satisfaction.

By the time the seventh and last inning arrived, we were winning 14–1, and the team from O.Z. was in total shambles. They had made several pitching changes without success. On offense, none of their batters had gotten farther than second base. To make matters worse, when one of their players was able to hit a hard drive to deep center field, Tommy stood on a park bench and caught the ball just as it was about to go over the fence. After that play, O.Z. looked totally defeated in body and spirit.

When their last hitter made the final out of the game, our players threw up their gloves, and Bo ran out from behind home plate to lift me in his arms, much in the way Johnny Roseboro of the Dodgers had done with Sandy Koufax in the final game of the '63 World Series. Then we went over to the O.Z. dugout to shake hands as an act of sportsmanship. While many of the players were gracious and congratulated us on our victory, a few turned out to be sore losers who were already heading out of the park.

When the handshaking was over, we returned to our dugout and lined up as Tommy distributed our winnings. Then we piled back into Eddy's car for the victorious ride home that felt like a ticker-tape celebration without the ticker tape or the parade.

Upon arriving back on the block, and in keeping with tradition, Pete, Davey, and I headed to the German deli to get sodas to celebrate. Winnings in hand, I splurged on a family-sized bottle of Hoffman's Cream Soda and a box of Devil Dogs.

The remainder of that night, as well as for the next several days, we all floated on cloud nine, recounting the successful journey that the ragtag Woodbine Street Squires had made into the land of O.Z.

Chapter XV

The Spiders and the Flies

Following our triumphant victory at O.Z., several guys from our crowd began to hang out with the Squires socially. Our attention shifted away from softball and onto the girls who stayed around the Squires and had come to watch the games. The specific focus areas of interest were named Genny, Donna, Carol, and Marie.

When the girls weren't at the softball field, they stayed down on Woodbine Street and Central Avenue, where most of the Squires lived. There was also another group of guys who hung out there. Unlike our new friends, these other guys were a bunch of sleaze balls whose idea of a good time was playing cards, drinking beer, and getting into fights afterward.

A week after the big game, hot and heavy rumors began swirling that several girls from the Squires had their eyes on a few guys from our block. The specific matchups were Donna and Pete, Marie and Davey, Carol and Timmy, and Genny and me. While the Squires couldn't have cared less, the "card sharks" down on Woodbine Street were less understanding because some of them had been dropped by the girls after we appeared on the scene. Unfortunately, we did not become aware of this until it was too late.

The girls from the field wasted no time making their

moves. Within a day of the rumors, they showed up on the block, supposedly passing through on their way to go window-shopping up on Myrtle Avenue. They were shopping, all right, but not on Myrtle Avenue and not in any windows. So as not to be too obvious, they travelled in pairs, approximately a half hour apart. The first night they showed up, Carol and Marie were the lead pair, followed by Genny and Donna a while later.

Once they appeared, they acted as though they were surprised to see us.

"Hi, Pete! Hi, Danny! How's it going?"

The old *How's it going* number. We had seen it before. Who did these girls think they were playing with—kids?!

"Hi, Donna. Hi, Genny," I said. "What brings you girls up around this neck of the woods?"

"Oh, we were just at the field and no one was there. Since it's a nice night, we thought we'd take a walk to Myrtle Avenue."

"You just missed Carol and Marie. They passed by a little while ago and were talking to Timmy and Davey. They must have gone up to Dairy Queen to get a milkshake."

"Is that so?" Donna responded, acting surprised.

During the subsequent conversation, Genny hung on every word I said. I knew what she was doing, but I got off on it anyway. Donna acted the same way with Pete. He played it cool, though, and told her he had to turn in and watch his brothers and sisters. After Pete was in his house, Timmy and Davey returned to the block, holding hands with the girls, laughing, giggling, and looking as though they were cats who had swallowed canaries. They stayed on the block for a while, then the girls proceeded on, but not before kissing Davey and

Timmy on the lips—right out in broad daylight!

As I headed home, Donna scurried ahead to catch up with Marie and Carol, but Genny stayed back and walked with me part of the way. I was really eating up all the attention, and before I knew it, I went for it.

No planning.

No strategies.

Just "Genny, would you like to go out with me?"

Followed by her simple response: "I'd love to!"

That was it!

The next day, I hurried to the block to brief Pete on the developments.

"Are you kidding?" he said. "Just like that? You asked her out?"

"Just like that!"

A few minutes later, Timmy and Davey joined us on Pete's stoop. They too wore broad grins.

"What are you two so happy about?" Pete said.

"Oh, nothing," Davey answered, giggling and poking Timmy.

"C'mon, c'mon, something's going on with you two. What is it?"

"Well," Timmy said, "Davey is smiling because he's going out with Marie."

"And Timmy's smiling," Davey chimed in, "because he's going out with Carol!"

"Hey, how about that!" I said. "I'm going out with Genny!"

"Hold on here, Mo, Larry, and Curly," Pete said. "Don't you guys think it's peculiar how in just one night those girls show up on our block, and you guys are already going out with them?"

"No," Davey said. "What's so odd about that?"

"You just have a suspicious nature, Pete," Timmy added. "That's all."

"Maybe I do, but the whole thing seems kind of fishy to me."

I mulled over Pete's comments. *Was he being too skeptical?* After all, we Woodbine Street guys were fast movers. Why wouldn't those girls want to go out with us as soon as we asked? Then again, it all had happened very quickly. *Nah, there wasn't anything going on.* Pete was just being overly cautious.

The next night, we all got together at the park.

Marie snuggled up against Davey on a bench in one of the dugouts. Carol and Timmy giggled nearby, and Genny and I sat in the bleachers holding hands while I figured out where we could go to make out in private. In the meantime, Pete spoke to Bo and Joe about setting up a return match with the guys from O.Z., and Donna stayed close by.

Nothing appeared unusual.

When it started to get dark, the girls told us they all had to be home early. Genny asked me if I could meet her on Central Avenue the following night. I interpreted the offer as a positive sign that we'd finally be able to go somewhere to make out.

After the girls went home, we returned to the block. During our conversations it became clear that Carol and Marie had made similar requests of Timmy and Davey.

After Timmy and Davey headed home, Pete and I sat on his stoop and talked.

"Something about those chicks leaves me with an uneasy feeling," Pete said.

"What makes you keep thinking that?"

"I can't quite put my finger on it. This whole situation happened too quickly, and now they want you to meet them in their neighborhood tomorrow night."

"Maybe they're getting tired of coming up to the field. This way we'll get to spend more time with them."

On the way home, I thought about Pete's suspicions but dismissed them. He was just overreacting.

The next night, I stopped off at the block before heading down to see Genny. Timmy and Davey had already left. Pete, however, had to babysit, and we talked about the situation briefly by his bedroom window. Before I left, he offered some final words of warning.

"Just watch yourself down there!"

"Okay, I will." Then I hopped off the stoop and headed toward Central Avenue.

The night was particularly hot. As I passed the softball field, I heard bongo drums coming from the far side of the park. There was an unwritten rule in the neighborhood that you didn't go into the park alone after a certain hour if you valued your safety. After dark, it belonged to the "Night Shift," a rough crowd of older teenagers who slept during the day and went to the park after hours to play cards, drink beer, smoke pot, and be "cool." The bongos were a warning signal that the Night Shift was on duty and all others should KEEP OUT!

I heeded the warning and hurried past the field, being careful to steer clear of any beer bottles that might have been thrown over the fence like human-seeking depth charges.

Five minutes later, I arrived at Central Avenue. Bo was in front of his house and welcomed me with the familiar "kick your ass" greeting. Across the street, Donna and Genny stood near a cellar door watching a card game. Davey and Timmy were also there making small talk with Marie and Carol. The guys playing cards had cigarettes dangling from their mouths and checked their hands through squinted eyes as smoke rose in their faces.

Charter members of the Mouseketeers they weren't. That was for sure.

I chatted with Bo and his girlfriend, Kathy, figuring Genny would come over once she saw me. To my surprise, she stayed across the street. The other girls stayed there as well. They all had odd, uneasy expressions on their faces.

Pete's warning echoed in my head.

As I talked with Bo, my attention split between our conversation and what was going on across the street. Thoughts kept running through my head. *How come she's not coming over? Why do she and the others have that look on their faces?*

I saw Davey try to put his arm around Marie as he said something to her. She pulled away, then shook her head as if to say no. She continued to watch the card game with her arms folded across her body. Timmy then turned and said something to Carol. She too responded in the negative. When he tried to hold her hand, she also pulled away.

A minute later I made direct eye contact with Genny. She turned and said something to Donna. Donna glanced in my direction, then turned back to the game. I wished I could read lips. Something was rotten about the whole situation, but I couldn't put my finger on it.

Suddenly, one of the cardplayers turned and said something to Davey, who replied. Then the guy got up and started pushing Davey around. Everyone got out of the way, and the cards flew all over the sidewalk.

"Uh-oh," Bo said in an ominous tone, "Davey better watch himself. That guy is a mean mother. He'll start a fight just for the fun of it."

Bo had barely finished speaking when the guy hauled off and nailed Davey squarely in the face. Another cardplayer then lunged at Timmy and pinned him against a wall.

I froze.

Part of me wanted to run across the street and do something—anything—to help my friends. Another part of me felt paralyzed with fear. These guys weren't fooling around, and I'd probably get my head smashed in. I grew incredibly angry. Davey hadn't done anything to his attacker. The guy had just been looking for an excuse to fight. Even more disturbing, it appeared that the girls knew something was going to happen.

The sixty-four-thousand-dollar question was, Why?

Davey picked himself up off the ground and made a feeble attempt to swing back at his assailant.

It was a mistake, a big mistake.

The guy wound up and smashed Davey again, hard. Very, very hard.

Davey went down, and the guy stood over him the way Cassius Clay had done to Sonny Liston in their second fight.

Blood poured from Davey's mouth and nose.

Meanwhile, Timmy flailed, still pinned and helpless against the wall.

These were my friends. I couldn't just stand by and watch; I had to do something!

"Bo, c'mon," I said. "Let's break it up!"

"Okay," he said, "but watch yourself."

We rushed across the street.

"Hey, what's going on?" I yelled, my voice cracking with fear and rage.

"Take your punk-ass friend and get out of here," growled the guy standing over Davey. "If we see you down here again, we'll break your heads!"

I wasn't about to argue with him. There'd be another time for settling the score. Right now, the most important thing was to get Davey back to the block in one piece.

Timmy was also released, and he helped me scrape Davey off the ground. Davey was hurt and angry. Despite his efforts to keep it together, tears flowed down his face. As we limped back home, I glanced over my shoulder at the girls. They just sat there on the cellar door, looking at the ground.

"Why? Why?!" Davey yelled when we were out of view of the others. "All I said to the guy was that he had a nice hand in cards. Then he gets up and takes a swing at me."

"Davey," I said, "there's more to what happened tonight than meets the eye. I don't know exactly what it is, but I'm sure going to find out."

The trip back to the block took thirty minutes. Periodically we stopped to let Davey compose himself and wipe blood from his face. Getting him cleaned up was a lot easier than convincing him not to turn around and go back to Central Avenue.

"I want to get that guy!" he screamed.

"Davey, not now!" I said. "There'll be another day for that. Let's just get you fixed up."

Rather than go directly to his house, we stopped by to see Pete, whose mother and father were still out. I rang his bell, and he peeked out through his bedroom window screen.

"Pete, it's Danny. Davey's hurt pretty bad. You got a wet rag and some ice cubes?"

"What happened?"

"Long story. Just help us get Davey patched up, and I'll explain later."

He left and returned to the window with ice cubes wrapped in a wet towel. As Davey applied the ice to his face, I explained things to Pete.

"Just like that, he hit you?" Pete said. "Did you do anything to provoke him?"

"Nope," Davey said, "I swear I didn't do nothing to him!"

"Where was Marie when this happened?"

"That's the odd thing. She was standing nearby but didn't do anything. A few minutes before, I asked if she wanted to go for a walk, but she told me she wanted to watch the card game. If we had left like I wanted to, the whole thing never would have happened."

Pete and I looked at each other. Pete then asked Timmy and me where we were when it happened.

"I was across the street talking to Bo," I said, "and Timmy was near the card players with Carol."

Pete turned to Timmy. "What did Carol do when the guy pinned you against the wall?"

"Nothing. Didn't even act surprised. She just stood there next to Marie."

"Something here doesn't sound right," Pete mumbled.

"I know what you mean," I said. "When I was across the street, Genny looked straight at me, then turned back to the card game. For someone who was so interested in me last night, she sure cooled off in a hurry."

"This whole thing smells like a setup," Pete said.

"Why would they do it?" Davey asked incredulously.

That was the big question.

It was getting late and we had to head home. Pete went back inside, and Timmy and I walked Davey home in case his mother started asking questions. It was dark and we hoped she wouldn't notice anything.

Unfortunately, it wasn't dark enough.

"David, what happened to your face?" she said immediately upon our arrival.

"Nothing happened to my face," Davey responded casually. "Whaddaya mean?"

"You're all scratched up. Did you get into a fight? Were you at the park? The neighborhood is changing. It's not safe down there!"

"Ma, I didn't get into no fight. I got hit in the face when we were playing ball."

"Why didn't you come home when it happened?"

"It wasn't that bad. It looks worse than it is."

Timmy and I did our best to back up Davey's story, and Davey's mother finally accepted our explanation, albeit reluctantly.

During my walk home, I replayed the scene in my head. When the guy jumped up and punched Davey, I'd felt fear and anger. *Should I have run across the street right away and gone after the guy? Had I acted like a coward when one of my friends had needed me?* The possibilities haunted me. *But the guy who went after Davey was a big dude and probably would have decked me as well. What good would that have done? Then Timmy would have had to take both Davey and me home. Besides, we were badly outnumbered. Plus, if I had been able to get the guy who hit Davey, there were three or four others who would have jumped in against me.*

Despite all the logical explanations I came up with, I still didn't feel comfortable. Maybe there was something I should have done and didn't.

It was late and I was tired. I just wanted to go home and get some sleep.

When I arrived at my house, my brother was already home.

"Hey, stud dud," he said, using his familiar greeting, "what's new with the lover boy?"

"Nothing much," I said in a subdued tone.

I didn't feel like talking, especially about the fight. If my brother heard what happened, he would want to go down to Central Avenue and break some heads. That was the last thing I wanted. It had been my fight, with my friends. I didn't need my older brother coming to my rescue. After all, no one had come to his rescue when he got into fights. I was determined to fight my own battles, even if it meant getting my ass kicked. I wasn't about to spend my life being protected by my big brother.

I went into the bathroom, turned on the faucet, and splashed cold water on my face. I leaned against the sink and hoped the water would wash away the bad memories of a few hours before. Later in bed, with my arms tucked under my head— my usual thinking mode—I analyzed the situation again, but my thoughts blurred as I drifted off into a deep sleep.

The next morning, I woke up early and got dressed. As I combed my hair, I took a long hard look in the bathroom mirror. *Had I punked out on Davey and Timmy the night before? Was there something I could have—should have— done but didn't?*

The thoughts nagged at me as I headed to the block.

When I turned onto Woodbine Street, I spotted Bo talking to Pete on Pete's stoop. I felt uneasy as I headed over to them.

"There he is," Bo said to Pete, following up with his familiar greeting of "kick your ass."

"You shoulda seen him," Bo said. "When Davey got hit, Danny threw down his newspaper and rushed over to break it up. I thought he might get hit too."

Bo's words put me at ease. Maybe I hadn't punked out after all. Feeling more relaxed, I went into more details about the night before.

Davey and Timmy soon appeared on Pete's stoop, both showing signs of wear and tear. Davey's left eye had a shiner on it, and his jaw was slightly swollen. Meanwhile, Timmy bore scratch marks on his neck from where he had been grabbed.

The five of us reviewed the events again, but we still couldn't figure out why it had all happened. It was like a puzzle with key pieces missing. We needed more information.

"Bo," Pete said, "is your girlfriend, Kathy, still talking to the other girls?"

"Yeah. They ain't best friends, but they do talk to each other."

"Do you think Kathy might be able to get us some information?" Pete asked. "We gotta be sure that the other girls don't find out we want it."

"Sure. If I ask her, she will. Besides, she doesn't like what they pulled."

After finalizing a few details, Bo headed to Central Avenue to find Kathy. The rest of us stayed on the block and maintained a low profile.

There was little feedback for the next few days, but Bo and Kathy finally showed up with some hot news. We headed to the knitting mill doorway to speak without interruption, huddling around Bo and Kathy.

"So, Kathy, what did you find out?" I asked.

"You're not going to like it."

"That's okay," Pete said. "Tell us anyway."

"Marie and Carol were going out with the guys who jumped Davey and Timmy," she said. "That is, they were going out with them until the night before the fight."

"How could that be?" Davey said. "We were going out with them for a few days before the fight."

"Well, it seems that Marie and Carol had been going out with those guys for a few weeks. But they didn't like the way they were being treated, so they decided to get even by breaking off with them and showing up with you guys. When Davey and Timmy showed up the other night and tried to hold hands and put their arms around Marie and Carol, it was like lighting a match to a stick of dynamite."

"I knew something smelled fishy," Pete said. "It all happened so fast! Those girls show up on our block, and in no time, they're going out with you guys."

"What about Genny and Donna?" I asked Kathy reluctantly.

"They were also going out with some guys from Central Avenue."

Pete and I just stared at each other.

The debriefing continued for a half hour. After the shocking truth settled in, we devised a plan to even the score.

With Kathy's help, we got word to Marie and Carol that Davey and Timmy wanted to talk to them. However, to avoid another confrontation on Central Avenue, we said that Davey and Timmy wanted to meet at a remote area of the softball field at the park. Once the time and place were confirmed, we had Bo get word to the guys on Central Avenue that we wanted a showdown with them at the same time and place.

We hoped to leave the rest up to the Night Shift at the park.

The night of the rendezvous, Pete and I headed to the field. From behind a concrete wastepaper basket near home plate, we surveyed the situation. We waited patiently and listened to the bongo drums coming from the far side of the park.

At nine o'clock, the girls came in through the right-field entrance.

I nudged Pete. "There they are!"

"Right on time."

Our eyes tracked the girls as they crossed the outfield and headed toward the designated location.

No sooner had their silhouettes faded into the darkness than the Central Avenue guys came in through the same entrance.

My adrenaline surged as the sound of the bongos grew louder.

We crouched down lower behind the wastebasket. If we were spotted, our asses would be grass.

The guys proceeded to the back of the field, their silhouettes also fading into the distance.

A minute passed before the bongo drums suddenly stopped, just like in the *Tarzan* movies before a major attack.

Loud voices, punctuated by screams from the girls, broke through the darkness.

"Get them!!!"

"Who are you guys?"

"Watch out behind you!"

"I think the guys from Central Avenue just got the official greeting from the Night Shift," Pete whispered.

"Yeah, wasn't that nice of them to do that?" I said. "I would love to stay around, but I think our mission here is finished. Let's get some sodas to celebrate."

"Sounds good to me."

We scurried out through a hole in the fence and sprinted up the block. When we reached the corner, we stopped at the German deli, bought some sodas, and returned to Pete's stoop.

Before long, we heard sirens. Then we spotted a police car turning the corner from Irving Avenue and racing toward the park. A second police car was hot on its trail.

"Whaddaya think is going on?" I asked Pete nonchalantly.

"I don't know, but those cops ain't heading down there to play softball. I think the girls and their playmates are getting a dose of their own medicine, big-time!"

"I only wish Davey and Timmy could have been with us to watch."

"In view of the fireworks going on, it's probably a good idea for us to keep tonight between the two of us."

"Good idea," I said.

We tapped our soda bottles to toast the success of our evening. "Mission accomplished, P.A." I said, using his initials.

"Mission accomplished, D."

We slapped each other five. Then he went into his house, and I took the long route home via Myrtle Avenue to stay clear of the police cars leaving the park, probably filled with guys from the Night Shift and Central Avenue.

As I walked home, I just enjoyed the weather—a beautiful summer night on which we had settled the score with the girls and their thug-bully boyfriends.

Other than Pete and me, no one else would ever know what happened. But that was the way we wanted it.

Once home, I went straight to bed and slept like a log, feeling like justice had been served.

The Flies had finally settled the score with the Spiders!

Chapter XVI

Breathing Lessons

After the saga of the Spiders and Flies ended, there were no more dramatic events with the crowd during the remaining days of the summer of 1964. However, there were numerous news reports in August about an international incident in which two American ships were attacked by North Vietnamese torpedo boats in the Gulf of Tonkin. It took place off the coast of a country very few of us knew about: Vietnam. Little did we know what impact that event would have on many of us in the future.

In September, our attention switched from the Squires and the Central Avenue crowd back to the block. Pete and Eileen were still going out together, and I, having fully recovered from my trouble with Genny, set my sights on Mary, the new friend of Eileen's from Bushwick.

As we had done in the past, Pete and I held strategy sessions about my latest romantic endeavor. Unfortunately, the situation with Mary was complicated because she liked Timmy. Timmy, on the other hand, was crazy about a girl named Diana, the sister of his brother's fiancée.

Timmy was so smitten with Diana that all he did was play Neil Sedaka's song "Diana" for hours on end down in the clubroom. She agreed to go out with him, but her feelings for

161

him were not as intense as his, and she broke off with him after only a short while.

Timmy had great difficulty accepting the breakup and asked Pete and me to confirm her feelings. He suggested we get the lowdown during Diana's next visit with her sister. We arranged it so we would all be in the clubroom with Diana, and when Timmy went upstairs to get sodas, we'd find out why she had broken off with him.

"So, Diana," I began, "how's it going with you and Timmy? The man has been on cloud nine since you two started going out together."

She looked surprised. "Didn't he tell you?"

"Tell us what?" I asked, feigning ignorance.

"We're not going out anymore. I like him as a friend, but not as a boyfriend. I'm surprised he didn't tell you."

"Maybe he felt it was only temporary and you two would get back together."

"Well, I hope he doesn't hold out hope, because we're not getting back together. But I don't want him to get hurt."

Pete and I looked at each other. Now the challenge would be to find a way to break the news to Timmy without getting him too upset. We had all been in situations like this before. No guy ever wanted to hear that the girl he was crazy about only "liked him as a friend."

"What have you all been talking about while I was gone?" Timmy said upon his return. He seemed to be suppressing a grin that betrayed his knowledge of our planned conversation.

"Nothing much," I said, hoping he would read between the lines.

"C'mon," he said. "I heard you all talking about something. What's the big secret?"

"There's no big secret," Pete said. "We were just making small talk while you were away. It's no big deal."

The situation felt awkward. Timmy knew what we'd planned to talk to Diana about. Now he was playing dumb and putting us on the spot in front of her.

"I think I know what you were talking about," Timmy said. "It's about Diana and me, right?"

What the hell are you doing? I thought. *We all planned this together!*

"I think there's some misunderstanding, Timmy," I said, trying to gracefully get us out of an uncomfortable situation. "Maybe we should talk later." I tried to convey a message with my eyes: *This ain't what you want to hear now.*

"No, I want to talk about it now! If you were talking about Diana and me, I want to know what was said!"

There was just no way we were getting out of this one.

"Timmy," Diana said calmly, "your friends were just telling me that they didn't know you and I had broken up. I was telling them that I like you as a friend, but not as a boyfriend."

"That's cool," Timmy replied. "I can dig it. What's the big deal?"

What's the big deal? Why the hell are we going through this little charade if it's no big deal?! I was not happy about the way we were being set up.

"I guess it's no big deal then," Pete said with a hint of sarcasm. "That's the end of that!"

When Diana left, Pete and I got Timmy aside. I felt like wringing his neck.

"Why did you set us up like that?" I said. "You knew we were trying to find out what was going on. Why make us look like a couple of jerks?"

"I had to hear it from her own lips. Otherwise, I don't think I could have accepted it."

"Okay, well why didn't you tell us that? We could have worked it out so that you heard what you needed to, without making us look like fools in the process."

While I felt bad for Timmy that his relationship with Diana had not worked out, I felt relieved that my situation with Mary might become more promising. If Timmy didn't make a move on Mary, she might become open to other possibilities, e.g., me. All I could do was wait and let nature take its course.

In the meantime, there were new rumblings about Pete and Eileen. Apparently, Eileen was having second thoughts about their relationship now that she was going to Bushwick, where new guys were giving her a lot of attention. She started sending Pete subtle hints that she might want her freedom, so Pete and I discussed the matter one night at his house.

We worked out a plan in which I would engage Eileen in conversation on the front stoop while Pete listened from his ground-floor bedroom window.

"Pete, just do me one favor when I'm talking to Eileen," I said.

"What's that?"

"Don't pull a stunt like Timmy did. If I get her to open up to me, don't pop your head out of your bedroom window and say, Surprise! or anything stupid like that. Okay?"

We both laughed and then I headed home.

The next night, we put our scheme into operation.

I finished my homework as soon as I got home, ate quickly, then headed for the block. As I walked there, I thought about what we were trying to do and laughed to myself. Better to get the giggling out of my system now rather than when I was with Eileen. I tapped on Pete's bedroom window, and his eyes peered through the small opening at the bottom.

"She should be out any minute," he whispered. "I told her I had some homework but that you wanted to talk over your Mary situation. Good luck!"

He ducked out of sight.

Wonderful. I'm supposed to talk to Eileen about Mary but also find out how she feels about Pete? This might be a little trickier than I thought.

A few minutes later, Eileen popped out of her front door with her usual serious expression.

"Hi, Danny."

"Hi, Eileen. How's it going?"

"Okay, I guess, and you?"

"Well, I'll know more after we talk," I said. "I'm not quite sure what the situation is with Mary."

"I know she likes Timmy a lot, but Pete told me about the discussion with Diana. Now it depends on whether Timmy is over Diana and is interested enough in Mary to ask her out."

"How long do you think Mary will wait for Timmy to show interest?"

"I don't know. I'll see her tomorrow in school, and if I get a chance, I'll find out."

While Eileen was talking, the wheels in my head were spinning as I tried to figure out how to shift the discussion to her and Pete. "Thanks, Eileen. How's school going, by the way?"

"Good," she said unconvincingly.

"What's the matter? You don't sound like you're having that good a time. Anything wrong?"

"No, I'm having a very good time. That's the problem!"

"You want to run that by me again?"

"Well, there are a lot of new guys I've met during change of class and at lunch period. Some are really nice, but they shut down once they find out I'm going out with someone, like I have some type of disease."

"Let me get this straight," I said to make sure that I (as well as Pete) was getting the story straight. "You feel tied down because you're going out with Pete? Is that it?"

"Sort of."

"Let me ask you this. Is there someone at school who you think you like?"

"There are a few guys I talk to a lot, but no one in particular."

"Have you talked to Pete about this?"

"Not really. I'm afraid if I tell him, his first reaction will be to break off with me. I'm not sure I want that either."

"It sounds to me like you want to have your cake and eat it too. Unless Pete knows the whole story, there's a good chance that you might break up anyway, with bad feelings on both sides. Later, you might find out that you really don't like any of the guys at school, but by then you also may have shut the door to getting back with Pete."

"I know," she said, looking as though I was getting through to her.

"I think your best bet is to level with Pete and tell him what you've told me. At least if you break up, you'll part as friends and not enemies. You'll also have a better chance of getting back together if you both change your mind."

"Yeah, I think you're right. I'll talk to him later tonight if I get a chance."

Having successfully carried out my mission, I figured it was time to head back home and give Eileen and Pete a chance to talk.

"Hey, look at the time!" I blurted. "I got to get going. Let me know how everything works out. Good luck!"

"Okay, I will. Thanks for all your help."

I hopped off the stoop and headed home feeling like I had masterfully handled the situation. Pete found out what he needed to know, and Eileen had an opportunity to sort out her feelings. They did wind up going their separate ways but also remained friends.

Several months passed, and by December the situation with Mary showed little promise. It seemed that she still liked Timmy, but he was still not over Diana. Meanwhile, Eileen spent more time with her new friends at school. One night during Christmas vacation, Pete and I were on his stoop in the freezing cold mulling over my situation. The problem clearly boiled down to finding a way to get Mary to come around. If she didn't, I'd have to move on to someone else. To take our minds off the cold, we reminisced about the schemes we had pulled off in Timmy's cellar and on the stoop with Eileen.

"To tell you the truth, Pete, at this stage of the game, I would settle for just making out with Mary. I mean, she doesn't have to go out with me. She can like Timmy if she wants to. I just want her body."

Pete and I laughed because we both knew there wasn't much more to Mary's thin body than there was to that of the Twins. In fact, from a distance it was almost impossible to tell Mary and the Twins apart.

"I would settle for making out with her—or anybody—at this point. It's been a while since I went out with Pam, and we didn't make out nearly as much as I would have liked."

"I know what you mean, D. Fortunately I didn't have that problem with Eileen. The girl loved to make out and knew what she was doing. She could probably give making-out lessons!" Then he tapped his temple. "You know, Eileen owes you a favor. You helped her break up with me so she could play the field at Bushwick. In the absence of anything happening with Mary, maybe she would help you by making out with you."

"I am always open to more instruction in that area," I added, smiling.

"You wouldn't be disappointed."

We sat quietly for a moment.

"I think she'd do it," Pete said, breaking the silence.

"Wait. You really do?"

"What have you got to lose by asking? All she can do is say no."

As if on cue, Eileen came out the front door. Pete and I looked at each other. He shrugged. I shrugged. Then he turned to face Eileen.

"Hi, Eileen, how's it going?" he said.

"Okay. How 'bout you?"

"I'm okay, but Dan here could use some help."

"With what?"

"Making out."

Eileen's eyes went wide as she turned to focus on me. "*Making out?* What kind of help do you need with making out?"

"Well," I said, trying to think and talk at the same time, "it's been a while since I made out with Pam, and if I go out with Mary, I don't want to blow it by messing things up when we make out. I could use some… practice and any pointers you might have from a girl's standpoint."

Pete chuckled and jumped in to help. "You know you're good at making out, Eileen, and it sure would be nice for you to help Dan."

Eileen looked surprised, flattered, and confused all at the same time.

"And if Mary ever loses interest in Timmy," I said, beginning to think that Pete and I were making a perfectly reasonable request, "I want to be ready."

"You know," Eileen said, "I've put in a good word for you with Mary. I've thrown your name around, like 'Hey! The guy you should keep your eye on is Danny. He's a lotta fun and pretty cute too!' She definitely knows you're around, but she needs more time to let go of Timmy."

"And when she does," I said, "it's all the more reason for me to be my best in the making-out department. It's the least I can do after all the trouble you've gone to."

"Okay, hold up," Eileen said. "Are you guys serious about this lesson thing?"

Pete and I exchanged a glance that counted for an entire deep conversation between close friends. Then at the same time, we both said, "Yeah."

"If I do it, it has to be just as friends, and it has to be a secret. I don't want anyone knowing and starting rumors that I'm some kind of slut."

"Absolutely," I responded. "This is just a friend helping a friend."

"Well," Pete said quietly, "it sounds like we've worked this out."

"Just one friend helping another," I repeated, my insides

already churning with excitement and anticipation. "Plus, by making out with me, you'll be helping two friends at once: Mary and me."

"Think about that," Pete said. "Mary will get the benefit of whatever pointers you give Dan. And Dan can pass those skills onto Mary."

"Okay, okay, let's not get carried away," Eileen said. "I said I would help Dan out. Let's leave it at that!"

"I agree with Eileen," I said, hoping to quit while I was ahead. I turned to her. "How about this? I'll meet you tomorrow night, and we'll make out for an hour or so. If you want to stop before then, we'll stop. Fair enough?"

"Okay, that sounds fair."

I couldn't believe this was happening. In less than an hour, the situation had gone from an innocent conversation about Mary to a planned make-out session with Eileen. Unbelievable!

For the next fifteen minutes, we agreed on conditions: no telling anyone, no do-overs, and no acting weird around each other after.

The next night, as I was getting ready to meet Eileen, my heart pounded a thousand beats a minute. This would be my first extensive plunge into making out marathon-style as opposed to the few kisses I had stolen from Pam.

On the way to the block, my feelings bounced back and forth between nervousness about what was in store and disbelief that Eileen was helping me out this way. When I turned the corner and scanned the block, I spotted her alone on her stoop. I headed over and tried to keep things relaxed and upbeat.

"Hey, Eileen, been waiting long?"

"No, I just came down two minutes ago."

No one else was around, which was good. Otherwise, there might be questions we preferred not to answer.

"Whaddaya say?" I said. "Ya want to get going?"

"Okay," she responded, seeming neither nervous nor regretful, which I took as a good sign.

In the interest of discretion, we headed for a spot near the railroad tracks a couple blocks away, where she and Pete had often gone to make out.

I made small talk as we walked. "Offer the lady my arm?" I said, trying to play it cool.

She looked at me and hesitated, but then she smiled, and we linked arms.

All systems appeared to be GO!

As we headed for the tracks, we ran into Joyce, an older girl who lived on the block. At twenty years of age, she was considered the wise older sister who sometimes counseled the Twins and Lisa in matters of the heart. When she saw us arm in arm, she looked at Eileen as if to say, What the hell is going on?

No time for chitchat, I thought. Better to keep moving before Eileen had time to change her mind. I moved us along quickly.

Ten minutes later, we reached the famous spot at the tracks. Based on the stories Pete had told me, I felt like I was entering sacred ground and even entertained thoughts of genuflecting. We headed for a secluded spot behind a freight car. Except for our legs, we were almost totally hidden from view.

As my heart rate soared even higher, I thought that it would be just my luck to have a heart attack before making out—and in a place where no one would find my body for days. Unless, of course, Eileen reported it. But I pushed the thoughts away and proceeded to the task at hand.

The moment of truth had finally arrived.

"Well, here we are," I said.

"Okay, Dan, lesson one. First you need to establish the mood. Then you've got to make the first move and not go in too strong. Start with lips only."

She leaned against the cold steel of the train, propped her foot against the surface, and waited expectantly.

"Got it!" I said. Then I moved in, assuming the mood in this case had already been firmly established.

During the first minute of making out, though, I found myself holding my breath. When we broke from the kiss, I held Eileen close and silently gasped for air. After ten or fifteen seconds, I regained my breath and dove back in. This time I breathed through my nose as we kissed.

That's it, I thought. *Now you're catching on. Slow, take it slow.*

After five minutes of kissing on the lips, I was ready for tongue kissing, and Eileen immediately responded.

Pete wasn't kidding. The girl knew her stuff!

During the tongue-kissing phase, I threw in a little body action. Slowly, ever so slowly, I rubbed her back. But it got a little complicated, rubbing with my right hand while concentrating on my breathing at the same time. After a few minutes, she reacted. Her breathing grew heavy, and she moved in on me, a positive sign that maybe she was getting HOT!

I opened my right eye to peek, which made the situation feel like a juggling act on the Sullivan show.

Kissing.

Breathing.

Rubbing.

Peeking.

Then, just as the breathing got heavier on both sides, Eileen broke the clinch.

"Danny, it's getting late. I think we'd better head back. You've been a very good student, and I don't think you'll have anything to worry about with Mary."

"A few more minutes and we'll go," I suggested, hoping to dive back in.

"I'd really like to go now. It's getting late."

I looked into her eyes and put a hand gently under her chin. "Absolutely, Eileen. Whatever you say. Thanks so much for helping me out!"

We walked back to the block in silence, but my mind raced.

I can't believe I pulled this off!

Unbelievable!

We rounded the corner and found the block deserted. When we reached her house, I broke the silence. "Thanks a lot for tonight. I really appreciate you helping me like this." Then I felt like I should throw something in about Mary. "If you see Mary tomorrow at school, tell her I said hello."

"I hope things work out between you two, Danny, and whatever you do, don't forget our agreement."

"Absolutely. Scout's honor!"

She waved and headed inside.

Unfortunately, I never did get to go out with Mary. But in all honesty, I didn't feel too torn up about it. Thanks to Eileen, I had finally broken the ice in learning how to make out and was ready and willing to move on to bigger romantic challenges with a new sense of confidence!

Chapter XVII

So Long, Annette Funicello

As the summer of 1965 approached, several of the guys on the block reconnected with a few members of the Squires for an outing to the World's Fair. It had opened the year before in Flushing, Queens, and would remain open for another year. The site was the same one where the 1939 World's Fair had been held twenty-five years earlier. Its return was widely publicized in local newspapers and on popular television stations.

With the arrival of the fair, the Flushing Meadows area of Queens was transformed into an international community of the future, where countries and companies from all over the world constructed elaborate pavilions and exhibits to showcase their cultures and visions of the future.

Several members of both crowds had already attended the Fair with their families, and based on our collective experiences, we compiled an itinerary of must-see events for our group field trip. Upon arriving, we had a difficult time deciding which pavilion to see first.

There were crowds everywhere.

A major frustration was our long wait at the most popular exhibits. At some, we found ourselves waiting outside for twenty minutes only to encounter another line once inside.

Although the average wait ranged from thirty to forty-five minutes, most of the presentations were worth it.

The first exhibit we attended took place at the Japanese Pavilion. Inside were hundreds of displays with futuristic-looking electronic devices ranging from small television sets to handheld radios and tape recorders. There was also a wide assortment of cameras demonstrated by attractive young Japanese women dressed as geisha girls.

The display with the televisions was roped off from the public and had a large sign in big block letters: PLEASE DO NOT TOUCH

For Pete, the sign was like waving a red flag in front of a bull. Before we knew it, he'd ducked under the rope and was turning controls and dials while muttering "Ha so" under his breath. The rest of us stayed a safe distance away while we laughed and kept a lookout for anyone who appeared to be a Japanese official. In a matter of seconds, Pete got a picture and sound on one of the sets. When the sound came on, a short Japanese man with a crew cut and three-piece suit came over and politely asked Pete to exit the display area. He showed Pete the sign, to which Pete responded with another muffled "Ha so." Then we scurried out of the pavilion, feeling it was best to leave voluntarily before we got thrown out.

Once outside, we headed to the next destination: the General Motors Pavilion, where we found an elaborate exhibit called the "World of Tomorrow." There we rode small golf-cart-like vehicles that transported two people at a time into a glimpse of the future. We wore headphones from which a deep voice, similar to that of famous news reporter Walter Cronkite, spoke to us. The voice guided us through an animated miniature exhibit below. It all looked so exciting as we observed small futuristic vehicles transporting people at supersonic speeds over modern "freeways."

Once that ride ended, we visited the Ford Motor Company Pavilion, which we found to be even more adventurous. Outside the pavilion, the newly introduced Ford Mustang was showcased. Inside, the tour was provided in late-model Ford automobiles that moved on a conveyer-belt device. At various points along the tour, exhibits were described through the car radio, which broadcast in a choice of several languages. Six of us crowded into a bright red Ford Galaxy convertible and directed Davey, who was in the driver's seat, to take us for a spin. Halfway through the tour, a minor scuffle broke out when Davey changed the language on the radio from English to Italian. By the time the skirmish was over, and the radio restored to English, Davey looked like he had been in a head-on collision.

After the Ford Pavilion, we experienced another lengthy wait to get into the General Electric Pavilion. There, we watched in amazement as a revolving stage with three animated mannequins described electrical appliances of the past, present, and future. Each time the stage revolved from one era to another, a cute jingle—"The Wonderful World of Tomorrow"—played over the sound system. The exhibit and the various scenes were fascinating, particularly in their portrayal of a modern, push-button, carefree future.

Afterward we stopped for a quick bite. Food and drinks at the Fair were outrageously expensive. A slice of pizza, usually thirty-five cents, cost more than twice that much. Hot dogs and other fast foods were equally overpriced. It seemed like many of the vendors were out to make as much money as possible, but with a lack of options, most patrons willingly paid their prices.

After gobbling down our food, we headed to the space exhibit, where life-sized models of rocket engines were on display. In addition, there were two space capsules: Friendship 7, the Mercury capsule in which John Glenn had orbited Earth three times; and a full-scale model of the larger, two-man Gemini capsule that would soon travel on longer missions. I was amazed at how small and cramped the Mercury capsule was. It looked like it could barely hold one person, and the control panel was a mass of switches and dials. The Gemini capsule, on the other hand, was roomier and almost twice the size. As I gazed at them, I felt a strong urge to climb inside just to get the feel of them. I thought that maybe someday, after becoming an electrical engineer, I would apply for a job at NASA and fly one of these babies myself!

Inside the space exhibit, we found a display illustrating the Apollo program, the third and final phase of the country's man-in-space program, upon which rested U.S. hopes of putting a man on the moon before the end of the decade to beat the Russians in the "race for space." The demonstration of the Apollo program was fascinating to watch, and during key times in the simulated landing and takeoff from the moon, I imagined what it would be like to go on such a journey. The simulation appeared so real that the crowd cheered when the model Lunar Module (LM) touched down, then applauded again when it lifted off from the surface of the miniature moon.

Toward the end of the day, after visiting most of the exhibits on our list, we walked around and took in some of the other sights. Pete and I got into a discussion about the changing situation on the block as it related to the girls. Eileen and Colleen had moved on to greener pastures at Bushwick, and only Lisa remained. Over the past couple of years, Lisa and I had gone out together several times during an on-again, off-again romantic relationship that was more off than on.

I really liked Lisa and thought she was very pretty, but our relationship had initially started with some drama. There had been a night on the block when no one was around except Lisa and me. We had a great conversation on her stoop, so just before she went in, I got this bright idea to ask her to go out with me. I didn't actually ask her but *told* her. She smiled broadly and ran into her house, almost tripping as she ran up the stairs. The next day, as I made my familiar trip to the block, I debated the previous night's spur-of-the-moment decision. While I liked Lisa as a person, there was the matter of her weight. But was that what really counted?

As I turned onto the block, I spotted Eileen on her stoop.

"I hear you and Lisa are back together," she said.

"The news sure travels fast."

"Half the neighborhood knows. First thing Lisa did this morning was go around to Pam's house to give her the good news."

"She *what*?"

"Yup, she gave Pam the good news and told her to make sure she kept her distance from you."

"She didn't."

"Yes, she did."

When I heard that, it became clear that my spur-of-the-moment decision was turning into a mess. While I had long written off any plans of getting back with Pam, I was not happy at all about Lisa talking to her.

"Where's Lisa now?" I asked, trying to conceal my anger.

"She and Colleen took a walk up to Myrtle Avenue. Lisa wanted to look at ankle bracelets."

Ankle Bracelets? Good God! That was like one step away from being married!

I'd made a BIG mistake. The situation had already gotten way out of hand, so I decided to put a stop to it and call it quits. I waited on Eileen's stoop for an hour as my mind raced between regret and outrage. When Colleen and Lisa finally turned onto the block, I hopped off the stoop and headed in their direction. After waiting for an hour, a minute more was too long.

Lisa had a big smile on her face, and Colleen wasted no time in congratulating me. Not knowing exactly how to respond, I just nodded and asked Lisa if we could take a walk.

I didn't want any witnesses around in case I decided to murder her.

We headed along Ridgewood Place by the lumberyard, and after two minutes of silence, I felt like we were far enough away. I got to the point.

"Lisa," I began tersely, "why did you go to Pam's house and tell her we were going out?"

Her smile faded. "I went there to tell her to keep away from you. That's why."

"What do you think I am? *Your property*? Just because I asked you to go out with me doesn't mean you own me. I think I want to call it quits!"

She stood there flabbergasted. An hour before, she'd been looking at ankle bracelets and now it was over.

"How come?" she yelled. "We are—or that is, *were*—going out. Why shouldn't I tell Pam to keep away from you? When she was going out with you, that's what she told me!"

"She *what?*" I asked, to be sure I was getting the story straight.

"That's right. When you were going out with Pam, she came around with Kathy and told me to make sure I kept my distance from you. So now that you and I are going out, I let her know the same thing."

"I didn't know that!" I responded in a less hostile tone. "But I still have second thoughts about our going out anyway. I like you as a friend, but I'm not sure I want to go steady."

"Okay, if that's the way you feel," she said, her voice cracking a bit.

The situation had turned into one huge debacle.

Those recollections crossed my mind as Pete and I continued our conversation at the Fair.

"I'm telling you, Dan, Lisa's weight is all baby fat," he said. "One day you'll see, and it may be too late. She's a pretty girl, and after she drops that weight, there'll be a load of guys beating down her door. You may find yourself waiting in line."

Having spent most of the day waiting in lines, the prospect of unnecessarily waiting in another one to see Lisa got my attention. I pictured how she would look with a knockout body, and images of the popular actress Annette Funicello ran through my head.

As my fantasies took over, I imagined walking down Woodbine Street with Annette Funicello on my arm.

Wow! Wouldn't that be boss!

Then dark images appeared in my mind as I pictured myself in a long line of guys waiting outside Lisa's house. She'd be looking out her window choosing her date for the night, and I'd be telling myself how stupid I was for passing up the ground-floor opportunity to go out with her when she was younger.

I still had my doubts, though, and pressed Pete further, as though he had a crystal ball. "How are you so sure it's baby fat? What if it's just plain old, regular, long-lasting fat?"

"Well, Dan," he said, imitating a wise sage, "if you want to know what a girl will look like when she gets older, all you have to do is look at her mother."

A picture of Lisa's mother, Fran, popped into my head. She was certainly attractive—and not an ounce of fat on her. Maybe Pete was right.

"How long you think it might take before Lisa starts looking like Annette Funicello?"

"Tough to say. Let's see, she's almost fifteen now. It might happen at sixteen or later."

Another year, possibly two, maybe even three? That was a long time. What if it was my luck that she took longer than that!?

"It's up to you," Pete said with an implied *I told you so* tone of voice.

The seed had been planted in my head. It was certainly something to think about.

That week, whenever I looked at Lisa, images of Annette Funicello ran through my head. And whenever Lisa's mother was outside, I scrutinized her—absolutely no fat!

I was in a real quandary.

Later that week, I asked Lisa out again. *Better to be safe than sorry.* The possibility of eventually going out with Annette Funicello was too much to pass up.

I was pleased and very relieved when Lisa agreed to go back with me. And if I wasn't mistaken, she was already starting to look a bit like Annette when she smiled!

"Way to go!" Pete said when I told him. "Just wait and see. You're making a smart move."

I hoped he was right. Anyway, in about a month we'd be returning to school. Lisa would be starting Bushwick, and I'd be in my senior year at Brooklyn Tech with tons of schoolwork. I'd see Lisa on weekends, time would start flying, and before I knew it, her transformation into Annette Funicello would be underway.

I just had to be patient.

Unfortunately, a week before school started, I got thrown for a major loop. Lisa informed me that she and her family were moving to Brentwood, Long Island, not far from where Pete's Uncle Eddy and Ralphie's family had moved several years before. Lisa's mother and father apparently felt concerned that the neighborhood was "changing" and that she and her younger brother, Sal, would be better off in the suburbs. While Lisa's father would have to work two jobs to afford it, her parents were firm in their decision and wanted to move quickly so that Lisa and her brother would start the new school year at Brentwood High.

The entire crowd, especially the Twins, were shocked and saddened by the news. Though we had missed Ralphie when he moved, we'd been much younger. This was different. The crowd had been together for years, with shared experiences that had brought us close together. For me, Lisa's moving seemed to be an ominous sign that Pete's prediction might come true. While I had made the smart move by asking her to get back together, fate was throwing me a curve ball. She'd probably turn into Annette Funicello, all right, but it would happen way out in Brentwood, which was practically God's country!

Just before Lisa's scheduled move date, I got to see her alone. She was terribly upset and felt that all her close friends were still right there on Woodbine Street. Plus, now it looked like she and I might finally wind up together longer than our average length of a week. She was angry at her parents because it was their idea to move, not hers. The neighborhood wasn't that bad, she reasoned. We'd all met a wide range of kids from other local neighborhoods over at Bushwick's night center, she said. What was the big deal?

Another major disappointment for her was that she wouldn't be attending Bushwick with the Twins. The three of them had often talked about how great it would be to be reunited in the same school, like the good ole days at St. Brigid's. Now that would all be changing. Lisa would have to start over again, making friends in a new neighborhood and school. At fifteen, that would not be easy.

The night before Lisa left, the Twins, Timmy, Pete, M.C., and I all sat with her on her stoop and reminisced about the ring-a-lievio games and the Bomber Party, which seemed like a long time ago.

An hour before she was supposed to go in, she and I took a walk. There was no one around. I held her hand and even dared to put my arm around her.

"Well, Lisa," I said, hoping reverse psychology would work, "what do you want to do? I don't want to tie you down."

"We can still write and talk on the phone," she said. "I'll try to come to the City when my parents visit my grandmother, and maybe you can come out to Brentwood to visit me too."

"Yeah, I'd like that! So, do you still want to go out with

me?"

"Sure, I do, Danny! I love you!"

"Well, that settles it then!"

I leaned over and gave her a long kiss on the lips. It was the closest we had ever come to making out. Then I walked her back to her house and waited outside until she appeared at her front window.

She waved to me and threw me a kiss while tears flowed down her cheeks. I waved back and returned the kiss. As I left her stoop, I walked backward to the corner so that we could continue making eye contact. Finally, at the corner, I blew one last kiss and turned to walk home.

So long, Annette Funicello.

I found myself wishing I could speed up time to quickly complete school, become an electrical engineer, marry my Annette Funicello, and live happily ever after in the suburban, push-button, modern world of tomorrow, just like the one I had seen at the World's Fair.

The question was whether my future would really turn out that way.

Chapter XVIII

Token Letters

New Year's Day 1966 ushered in a new mayor, John Lindsay, and a transit strike. Lindsay was young and good-looking and often compared to John Kennedy. Despite being a Republican in a traditionally Democratic city, he got elected, which many attributed to his support from women voters.

No sooner had Lindsay taken office than he faced a major crisis in the form of the first transit strike in the City's history. Thanks to the strike, the daily routine of the City came to a screeching halt. I was in my senior year at Tech, getting ready for midterms. In response to the strike, the Board of Education instructed all students to go to their local neighborhood schools, which in my case meant Bushwick.

The first day, I showed up at Bushwick's auditorium promptly at 8:30 a.m., as directed. It was a real treat going to school with M.C., Timmy, and the Twins. The principal at Bushwick had expected only a handful of kids from other schools and was totally unprepared when a hundred and fifty of us showed up. To deal with the unexpected crowd, an ad hoc system was implemented in which students from outside schools buddied up with a comparable-level classmate from Bushwick. My Bushwick buddy turned out to be a guy who was doubling up in history and English and repeating plane geometry for the third time, which I found amusing.

While Bushwick did little for me academically, the more relaxed, coed social environment was a nice change from Tech, which was a nose-to-the-grindstone, all-boys school. I particularly enjoyed the change of classes, during which I got a chance to check out the girls. Occasionally, I bumped into Mary and the Twins in a stairway or at lunch, and I quickly found that most of the Bushwick kids had a more casual attitude about school than I did. The girls spent much of their time fixing their makeup and teasing their hair. For most, their main life objective was to graduate, become secretaries, get married, have kids, and then retire from ever working again.

Most of the guys also viewed school as a necessary evil, and while a few planned on attending college, the majority looked forward to getting blue-collar or civil service jobs after graduation and then buying a "hot set of wheels."

Outside of our immediate environment and halfway around the world, the situation in Vietnam continued to heat up. Almost every night, television news clips reported rising numbers of American soldiers running through jungles or crouching behind grenade launchers. Though it still seemed unreal, there were increasing signs in the neighborhood that the war was coming closer to home as more front windows displayed small American flags, proudly inscribed with the words "In Service."

It also seemed like more of the neighborhood guys who had graduated high school a couple of years before us were getting drafted. When home on leave after basic training, many could be found up at the Grove Billiard Parlor in their dress uniforms, sharing stories of military life with friends who would soon find themselves in similar situations.

Lefty, the manager of the pool room, erected a large wall sign wall listing the names of neighborhood guys in service and their respective branches. Later, a gold star would be placed next to the names of several who didn't make it back.

In April, a very official-looking envelope from the Defense Department arrived for my brother. Inside was a letter instructing him to appear for a physical examination at White Hall Street in Manhattan. He was nineteen years and five months old, several months younger than many in the neighborhood who were getting drafted. In addition to the letter, the envelope contained two transit tokens, one to get him to White Hall Street, the other to get him home. If he passed the physical, the next letter would contain only one token along with orders instructing him to appear for induction.

For most of the eligible guys in the neighborhood, getting drafted was inevitable. There were very few in our blue-collar, lower-middle-class neighborhood who would ever consider evading the draft, because many of their fathers had fought in World War II. The view of many was that the U.S. was in South Vietnam to protect Southeast Asia from the threat of Communism. According to the Domino Theory, which we heard so much about in the news, if South Vietnam fell to the Communists in the North, the rest of the neighboring countries would soon fall like a stack of dominoes—and if that happened, the Communists would be at our doorsteps in California. The Communists were already in Cuba, where we'd sweated out the missile crisis years before; that had been bad enough. So, for most of the guys from the neighborhood, the draft was a call to defend their country. Most would do their two years of service (or more if they enlisted) and then hope to get on with the rest of their lives when they returned home.

Patriotism aside, the most troublesome aspect of the draft was the limbo it created in young men's lives from the time they turned eighteen and had to register for the draft until the time they actually got drafted. This issue became a frequent topic of conversation between Pete and me over egg salad sandwiches at Kolletty's Ice Cream Parlor on Myrtle Avenue.

For me, the issue of going into the service was many years away. I planned to graduate Brooklyn Tech that June at the age of sixteen, and I hoped to get accepted into City College's engineering program in the fall. If accepted, I would be a sophomore by the time I got my draft card at eighteen. As a full-time college student, I would have a 2-S draft deferment classification until I graduated the five-year electrical engineering program in 1971 at the age of twenty-one. Although it all seemed far off in the future, I still felt like the service was an inevitable obligation I would have to fulfill. By the time I graduated college and completed two years in the service, I'd be twenty-three. Through the eyes of a sixteen-year-old, that seemed like a long time away. Pete, on the other hand, was in a different boat. He had already graduated high school, turned eighteen, and worked for almost a year. He had trained to be a plumber in high school, but after a few months as a plumber's assistant dealing with leaky faucets and clogged toilet bowls, he had changed his mind and taken a job at a bank in downtown Manhattan. He was also taking an accounting course in the evenings after work at nearby Pace University.

"If I wasn't going to college and was eighteen, I'd probably join the Air Force or the Navy," I said to Pete while chomping on my egg salad sandwich one day. "At least there's a good opportunity to get an education, something you can use when you get out."

Logical, very logical—that was me, all right. Besides, I liked the style of the blue Air Force uniforms more than those from the other branches.

"The only problem with that," Pete said, "is that the Air Force is a four-year hitch. That's a long time to spend in the service. If I had to go in, I'd go into the Navy. It's a three-year hitch and you get a chance to do some traveling."

"Yeah, I can dig that," I said as pictures of tropical islands, swaying palm trees, and dancing island girls floated through my head.

Then I told Pete about my brother getting the letter with the two tokens in it. "If he passes the physical, he figures he'll be getting called for induction in August or September."

A brief silence followed.

Pete was exactly one year younger than my brother. In a year or so, he'd be going through the same ritual: the letter with the two tokens; the physical; and then, most probably, the letter with a single token.

I could see his mind working. Financially, it was impossible for him to attend college full-time and be eligible for the 2-S deferment. As with my brother, between now and the time Pete turned nineteen, his life would be in a holding pattern. Fortunately, however, Pete's job at the bank would be waiting for him when he got out of the service. That was more than many guys in the neighborhood could count on.

After we left Kolletty's, we walked around Myrtle Avenue debating our respective strategies for winning the war. It seemed like the more North Vietnamese that got killed, the more there were to replace them. We had talked about it briefly at school. It was clear that the North Vietnamese were getting aid from the Red Chinese and the Russians. With the U.S., the Chinese, and the Russians all having "the bomb," it looked like the confrontations between the superpowers were going to take place in these smaller countries, as had been the case in the Korean Peninsula.

From what I had seen on the nightly news, I figured the Air Force was the key to winning. If the U.S. got tied down in ground fighting, the North Vietnamese would have the advantage. We all knew it was always better to fight on your own block, a lesson we'd learned well from the Central Avenue incident.

A week later my brother received another letter informing him that he had passed the pre-induction physical. Now there were no doubts about his near-term future. It was just a matter of time. With my parents' approval, he started to stay out late on weekends, intent on squeezing in as much fun as he could before Uncle Sam called.

A few weeks later, his induction letter arrived.

I had just returned home from school to find my mother sitting at the small red-and-white metal kitchen table that had been in our family since my brother and I were small children. She was sobbing.

No sooner had I closed the door behind me than she pointed to an envelope on the table from the Defense Department.

"I think your brother got his draft notice," she sobbed, barely able to control herself.

Initially, I just looked at the envelope. Then I picked it up and felt for a round, coinlike object. There was something in there, all right. I kept my hopes up that perhaps it was just a paper clip.

At 5:30 p.m., my brother arrived home from work, still dressed in his mechanic's coveralls. As soon as my mother saw him, she cried again and went into the bathroom. I handed my brother the envelope and communicated with him via a silent glance.

He took the envelope and, prior to opening it, examined it with his fingertips much the way I had.

By this time, my mother had returned to the table.

My brother carefully opened the envelope to avoid ripping any of its contents. He removed the letter and read it to himself. From where I sat, the letter appeared to be typed in a block style.

Very neat.

Highly organized.

Very official.

After reading the letter to himself, my brother whispered, "This is it."

Then he reread it aloud. "Private John Joseph Holford, Jr., having successfully passed the pre-induction physical exam, this letter is to inform you that you are to report to the Army Induction Center on White Hall Street at 0800 hours on September 10, 1966."

The letter went on to instruct him to bring a change of clothing and other items like shaving equipment, etc.

"Well, I'm on my way!" he announced, taking a surprise punch at my arm, as he had done dozens of times before. I didn't mind it, however. In fact, I was going to miss them.

Later that evening my father arrived home. My brother showed him the now-familiar letter, and they talked a bit about my father's days in the Navy during World War II. Back then, when my father had enlisted, the country was in a full-scale war with guys eager to sign up. In contrast, the situation in Vietnam was very murky.

School ended a week later, and I graduated Tech. Based on my grades and SAT scores, I was officially accepted into City College's engineering program, which I would begin that September.

The day after I graduated Tech, Pete and I got together for another marathon egg salad sandwich eating session up at Kolletty's. When we entered the ice cream parlor, he told me he had something to talk about, so we settled into our usual booth in the rear. As we waited for the waitress to take our order, I told Pete about my brother receiving his induction notice.

Then he dropped a bombshell of his own. "Dan, I've got something to tell you."

"Okay, who are you in love with now?"

"No, it's not anything like that. I'm going into the service."

His words had just rolled out, barely louder than a whisper.

"You're what?"

"I've enlisted in the Marines," he said more audibly.

I wasn't sure which word was more shocking—*enlisted* or *Marines*!

"IIow come?"

"Well, I went down to see this recruiter last week, and he offered me this great deal. It's a two-year enlistment and they'll also send me to school."

"How come you didn't go into the Navy?"

"The Navy is a minimum of three years. I don't want to be tied up for that long. Besides, I want to prove to myself that I can do it."

"Do what?"

"That I can make it through the training. The Marines are the toughest. I have to find out if I can take it."

I couldn't believe my ears.

My grandfather had served in the Marines during World War I. When my brother and I were young, he used to tell us about his days in "the Corps," and he'd show us the good conduct medal he had earned. Up until the age of sixteen, my brother had talked about how someday he'd become a "leatherneck." But as he'd approached draft age, his enthusiasm for the Corps dwindled, particularly as guys from the neighborhood returned with horror stories about Marine Corps boot camp.

Despite those stories, my best friend was now going into the Marines. It felt like a bad dream.

We had another round of sandwiches, then walked around Myrtle Avenue for a while. I asked Pete about his family's reaction to his enlistment.

"My father isn't thrilled about the idea, but he told me that if it was something I wanted to do, he wouldn't stand in my way. My mother is taking it very badly. She just keeps asking me if there was something she did or didn't do to make me want to enlist."

Afterward, Pete filled me in on the deal he had been promised. "First, I go to boot camp down in Parris Island, South Carolina. Later, I'll be sent for advanced training, where I'll also have a chance to go to school in my free time."

After advanced training, the next stop would be anyone's guess. From the sounds of the evening news, chances were exceptionally good that it would be Vietnam.

That prospect, however, still seemed far away.

While Pete's decision to join the Marines initially appeared to be impulsive, the more he explained, the more rational it seemed. "In a year or so, I'll get drafted into the Army anyway, and between now and then, I'll just be marking time. Once I do get drafted, I'll probably wind up in Vietnam. This way, I have control over my life, and if I do go to Vietnam, I'll go with the training from the Marines rather than the Army."

There was little in his thinking I could disagree with. In addition, the Marines had offered him a delayed enlistment, meaning he didn't have to leave until late August. That would give us a couple of more months to hang out together during the summer, probably for the last time in a while.

We immediately focused on plans to make it the best!

Chapter XIX

Good Vibrations

During the next several days, Pete and I spent a lot of time discussing the best ways to spend the last summer before he went into the service and I started college.

Most of the crowd from the block had drifted off in different directions. Lisa was in Brentwood, the Twins had moved to Staten Island, M.C. had hooked up with a crowd from Palmetto Street, and Timmy was going out with a girl who lived several blocks away.

The novelty of shooting pool up at the Grove and hanging out at Koletty's had faded. Although neither of us had a car, we did have money—Pete from his full-time job at the bank and me from a part-time job at a local department store.

"Let's face it, Dan, the situation on the block is dead. We gotta branch out, find new action."

"You're right, and we gotta move fast!"

The immediate challenge was finding out what action was happening and where. Unless you belonged to a crowd, it was difficult to get the scoop on what was going on.

Oddly enough, we didn't have far to look.

One night after shooting pool, we detoured past Madison Street, a block adjacent to Woodbine Street. On the stoop of the corner house on Madison Street and Ridgewood Place were three girls we recognized from Sunday Mass at St. Brigid's. Now further along in our adolescence, we felt more socially sophisticated than when we had innocently and discreetly checked them out during Holy Communion.

We headed in their direction and exchanged hellos with Cathy, Bunny—Cathy's older sister—and a friend of theirs named Little Ann. Although we had seen the girls around the neighborhood, we'd never interacted with them—until now.

We made small talk and asked them where they had been hanging out.

"Either in Putnam Park, right behind Bushwick's softball field, or at the Marteen Club," Cathy said.

Pete and I were well aware of the Night Shift at Putnam Park, who had unknowingly taken care of the Central Avenue guys the summer before. The Marteen Club, however, was something new. When it was mentioned, Pete's eyes lit up.

"Hmm," Pete said, "the Marteen Club. What's that?"

"It's a social club run by St. Martin's Church down on Hancock Street," Bunny replied.

"On weekday nights, kids get together in the church basement to listen to records on the jukebox, shoot pool, play ping-pong, or work out. They also hold dances in the school gym on Saturday nights."

"Do you have to join anything?" I asked.

"Nah," Cathy said. "The church sponsors it as a way of keeping kids off the streets and out of trouble during the summer. We're going tomorrow. Why don't you join us?"

"We may do just that," Pete responded casually.

It was getting late and I had to head home, so I took off.

"I'll talk to you tomorrow, Dan," Pete said.

I knew that meant that we would have one of our famous

egg salad sandwich debriefing sessions at Koletty's.

The next day, Pete filled me in. "This may be the situation we've been looking for," he said excitedly. "I spent almost two hours with those girls. Sounds like this Marteen Club has possibilities. We got nothing to lose. I told them we'd meet them by their house at seven thirty tonight. We'll walk there with them and check it out."

We dressed casually for the evening, but better than we did during the day. I even spritzed myself with some Canoe cologne that I'd received the month before as a graduation gift. The girls looked good, wearing casual but dressier clothing along with makeup.

St. Martin's Church was a fifteen-minute walk from the block, so we used the time to get more information from the girls on what to expect.

"Basically, it's a pretty good crowd of people," Cathy said. "Some couples stay to themselves all night, but most people are friendly. In the early part of the night, a lot of the guys shoot pool and hit punching bags while the girls listen to the jukebox in the cafeteria and talk about guys they're going out with or want to go out with. Eventually, the guys come to the cafeteria and dance with the girls. By the end of the night, the stage is pretty much set for who will be with whom at the dance on Saturday."

It sounded like the rituals we had performed back on the block during games of ring-a-lievio and payoff.

Different age.

Slightly different game.

Same goal.

When we arrived, a crowd of people were hanging around outside. Some guys were hitting harmony and sounded good.

A few others leaned against cars, and a guy who could have passed for Ed "Kooky" Burns from the *77 Sunset Strip* television show was sitting in a sharp-looking bronze '57 Chevy convertible. Its white top was pulled down to expose a custom white rolled-and-pleated Naugahyde interior. The car was like honey to several girls, who buzzed around like bees.

The girls we were with knew everyone and introduced us. Most of the crowd was friendly, and in no time at all we were making small talk about where we were from and how we knew the girls. We made it sound like we had known them forever. Overall, there was a feeling of electricity in the air and a sense that we were at a real happening.

As we worked the crowd with the girls, moving from new acquaintance to new acquaintance, Pete slipped his hand behind his back, and I slapped him five.

"Good vibrations," I said, referring to the song the Beach Boys had just released.

"Good vibrations," Pete responded.

After twenty minutes of hanging out in the street, the crowd moved inside and down a long flight of narrow stairs to the school basement. The building was only six or seven years old, and the basement was painted in modern bright blue, white and light green colors, with matching floor tiles. There was also a drop ceiling and recessed lighting operated by dimmer switches. Two large metal double-doors led to an open area that served as the cafeteria during the school year. Most of the folding tables had been put away for the summer, and the open area served as a perfect dance floor. A brightly lit Wurlitzer jukebox was strategically centered against a rear wall, and coincidentally, "Good Vibrations" greeted us as we entered.

The girls gave us a tour. Adjacent to the large cafeteria area were two small older-looking rooms that had been part of the basement where the old church and newer school joined. Walking from the cafeteria into the rooms of the church basement felt like taking a trip back in time. In contrast to the modern school, this area had high arched limestone ceilings dimly lit by suspended swag-lights encased in stained glass. In the center of one small room was a full-sized pool table with faded green felt cloth.

The other room was set up as a workout room with mats, weights, and two punching bags suspended by chains that must have previously supported the heavy light fixtures.

At the end of our tour, we emerged back into the brighter cafeteria, where we subtly checked out the girls and tried to determine who was attached and who wasn't.

Eventually, the guys came into the cafeteria to talk to the girls. Cathy, Bunny, and Little Ann sat with Pete and me to brief us further on what was going on.

"This is the time of night when people start checking each other out. The girls have already figured out who they're interested in. If the wrong guy is hanging around them, they'll go to the bathroom and change seats when they return. If the right guy is hanging around, then a friend will get up to make a seat available."

Spiders and Flies, I thought. The guys think they're making the move, but all they're really doing is walking into a web being spun for them.

"After a while," Cathy continued, "couples will start dancing. In the early part of the night, mostly fast songs get played, but once people have warmed up to each other, slower songs come on."

I nudged Pete. "Sounds like the old days during the Bomber Party. Fast songs in the beginning of the night, slower songs later."

"Yup, except these girls look a lot better than the Twins and Lisa ever did."

"That's the difference," I said. "Back in those days, the Twins and Lisa were girls. These girls look more like young women." They certainly did, dressed in tight jeans and blouses that left little to the imagination. Some of the girls wore clingy miniskirts, dark stockings, and heavy makeup. While some were not very pretty, the short skirts and dark stockings got our attention. Cathy referred to them as "back-seaters."

"Why do you call them that?" Pete asked.

"Because when they leave here, they'll wind up in the back seat of some guy's car."

"Just my luck," I said to Pete. "I don't have a car!"

After the music played for a while, Little Ann asked Pete if he wanted to dance. As I watched them dance, I thought to myself that things were moving along quickly. Just a week before, Pete and I were sitting on his stoop trying to figure out how to make this summer one to remember. Now we were in this new place with this new crowd, with unknown possibilities ahead. When I came back to the present, a slow song came on the jukebox, and it looked like Little Ann had no intentions of sitting down. I couldn't hear what she was saying to Pete, but he kept smiling. As they whirled around on the dance floor, Pete winked at me and raised his eyes upward. Little Ann had both arms around him, and as Timmy's mother would have said, There was little room between them for the Holy Ghost.

I glanced around the large cafeteria to see the scene

repeated several times over. The lights had been turned down and the place was getting hot, both literally and figuratively, so I went to the bathroom to throw cold water on my face. Pete eventually came in, scanned the area, and saw that we were alone.

"Isn't this great!" he said. "This was exactly what we wanted: new crowd, new action, and new women!"

"It sure is different. Looks like you're doing okay with Little Ann. Are you walking her home?"

"I think so. That chick is something else. She was asking me all kinds of questions about whether I'm going out with anybody, and how she used to check me out whenever I walked by her pew at St. Brigid's. She even wants to know if she can give me a hickey for luck to start the summer!"

"I'd love to see the look on your father's face when you get home with a big red love bite on your neck!"

Pete laughed and we headed back out. Pete decided to walk Little Ann home, but I planned to stay a while longer and check things out. We agreed to catch up on the block the next day.

After he left, I stayed with Cathy and her sister. They were checking out two guys but were disappointed when they left with two back-seaters. After that, they asked me if I wanted to go, but I opted to stay and check things out a little longer.

I headed to a room where three guys—Russ, Neil, and Jackie—were shooting pool. They were friendly and asked me to join them. They were around eighteen, and Jackie and Neil had both gotten cars for the summer. Russ was taking his road test that next week. Not knowing my age, they asked if I drove. I told them I had my permit and was hoping to get "wheels" for the summer if I could afford the insurance. First-year drivers were usually put into a high-risk pool by insurance companies, and the premiums were extremely high. I had found this out when my brother got his license and complained about the three-hundred-dollar charge for insurance.

The closest I would come to getting wheels that summer would be weekend driving lessons from my brother in a deserted industrial area in Maspeth, Queens, where he had learned to drive. And that was only if my father didn't find out about it. My brother had given my father more than a few gray hairs when he learned to drive, and my father never completely got over my brother taking his beloved '51 Dodge to the Islip speed track, where he'd raced the car and blown up the engine. He wasn't looking forward to similar possibilities with me. I also hadn't helped my case the summer before when fixing the radio in my father's car. I'd attempted to move the car ever so slightly in its parking place, and I'd almost smashed another car when I let out the clutch too quickly and the car leaped forward. Luckily, my father's car stalled out before making physical contact.

This reality notwithstanding, I did take comfort in feeling accepted by these new acquaintances and their assumption that I was their peer, when, in fact, I was only sixteen.

After a few games of eight ball, Russ suggested we go for a couple of beers at a local bar, the Half-Moon Inn.

Jackie and Neil agreed and asked me if I wanted to join them. I said, "Sure, why not?" while wondering if I would get served. The legal drinking age was eighteen, and bars usually asked for a draft card as proof. If I went, I'd have to bluff my way in by acting older, like I had when I'd gotten into the Grove Pool Room at fifteen. Most of the guys I graduated with were eighteen, so I figured I could use my high school ring as proof of age. If challenged to produce a draft card, I'd claim not to have my wallet on me and act insulted at having to produce it in the first place. It was all about the bluff.

We drove to the bar in Neil's old black-and-white four-door 1958 Ford Galaxy. Russ sat in the front with Neil and Jackie, and I rode in the back. While the car's glory days were behind it—showing signs of exterior body rot in a few places—it was still in pretty good shape, enhanced by Neil's attempts to spruce it up with bright red terry-cloth seat covers and matching floor mats.

As we rode, we complimented Neil on his wheels and kidded him about how it had probably helped him score with his fair share of back-seaters.

"I only hope I can add a few more back-seaters to the history of this old car before it goes to junkyard heaven," he joked. When we arrived at the Half Moon Inn, we entered in single file. I picked the third position, behind Russ and Neil, with Jackie to my rear. There were no other customers in the dimly lit bar. Russ exchanged greetings with the bartender, a big, burly, mustached guy named Bill who was the spitting image of a bartender. Russ introduced us and ordered four beers. As the others pulled up stools, I watched them take out five-dollar bills and place them on the bar. I did the same, doing my best to act relaxed. *Just another night out with the boys at the bar.*

As we munched on pretzels and sipped our beers, we decided to play shuffleboard. I had watched my father play years before at Connell's and was familiar with the game and its scoring. Russ put a few quarters in the jukebox and asked for requests. I recommended "Good Vibrations" while the others asked for songs by the Beatles, Rolling Stones, and Supremes. After scanning the list of songs, Russ let out a loud roar to Jackie and Neil.

"Hey, looky here. Bill got in our favorite song."

"'The Mouse?'" Jackie asked.

"'The Mouse!'" Russ replied.

Then the three of them started singing about doing the mouse in their house.

Soupy Sales, an extremely popular television performer, had created the song and its accompanying dance. He was famous for throwing—or getting hit in the face with—cream pies. He also had several puppet characters on his show, two favorites of which were White Fang and Black Tooth.

As the song blasted, Russ, Neil, and Jackie stopped playing shuffleboard and started dancing around the bar. When it ended, they resumed their game as though nothing had happened.

After four rounds of beers and several plays of "The Mouse," we called it a night. Each of us left a tip on the bar, a "bill for Bill" as Russ described it, and then we headed out. The night air felt good but only served to exaggerate the smell of cigarette smoke on our clothing, so we rode with the windows open while singing "The Mouse" and doing our best imitations of White Fang and Black Tooth. If we'd had a pie in the car, someone would have gotten hit in the face with it.

When we arrived at my house, we exchanged White Fang and Black Tooth farewells and agreed to meet at the Marteen Club the next night. Then Neil peeled out, and I headed inside, sniffing my clothes for telltale signs of my excursion. Fortunately, my mother was sleeping, so I quickly changed and buried my clothing at the bottom of the laundry hamper in the bathroom.

The next day, Pete and I shared our experiences. I gave him the scoop on my outing, and he had lots to share about his walk home with Little Ann, which took an hour and a half.

"We must have made out in the doorways of twenty houses on the way home," he said.

Apparently, the Woodbine Street crowd wasn't the only one to use doorways for making out, and from Pete's description of Little Ann's skills, it sounded like she was no stranger to cellar doorways. During most of that summer, Pete and I spent a large part of our time with the crowd from the Marteen Club. We made good friends, and Pete and Little Ann developed a hot on-again, off-again relationship. I had a few brief flings with Cathy but nothing steady. Several of the guys purchased cars, so we frequently went on outings to Brighton Beach and other places.

In addition to the weekly activities, dances were held every Saturday night with live bands made up of local neighborhood guys who also belonged to the club. Everyone got dressed up for the dances, and the gymnasium was decorated with balloons and twisted crepe paper. The floor was liberally sprinkled with sawdust to protect it from the onslaught of high heels and leather soles. The lighting was also dimmed to minimize the ravages of acne and make everyone look good.

A ritual that many participated in prior to the dances involved getting drunk. Someone usually brought a pint bottle of rum, rye, or vodka, mixed with coke, ginger ale, or orange juice. The drinking took place an hour before the dance to allow enough time for it to take effect.

"Good Vibrations" in a bottle, as they described it.

Although Pete and I were having a blast hanging out with

this new crowd, we had reservations about drinking. The Woodbine Street crowd had been very straight. Except for Timmy, none of us smoked, and our only exposure to alcohol had been a special occasion when M.C. confiscated a bottle of homemade red wine from his grandfather's basement.

To deal with the peer pressure from the Marteen Club crowd, Pete and I told them that we drank before we left the block. The truth of the matter was that we didn't drink at all, but we acted like we did by slurring our speech. Since most everyone else really was high, they didn't think otherwise. When the others looked as though they were sobering up, Pete and I also "sobered up." We even developed reputations as being able to hold our liquor well, which we laughed about on our walks home. During these walks, we also shared our observations about how people changed after they got buzzed, particularly the quiet ones who suddenly became party animals!

Over the course of the summer, I became increasingly curious about what it would feel like to get buzzed and experience "Good Vibrations" in a bottle, so before the last dance of the summer, I purchased a half pint of 104 proof Southern Comfort bourbon, which I hid in my basement. Before the dance, Pete and I quietly detoured to my cellar, leaving the light off so as not to draw attention. I fumbled around in the damp darkness and finally found the small bottle.

I broke the seal covering the cap and carefully opened it so as not to spill any on my clothing. It smelled and tasted like medicine. I took a few swigs, but since we weren't sure what the effects would be, we decided that one of us would not drink. We tiptoed up the cellar steps and listened for any traffic in the hallway. It was quiet, so I slowly opened the door and peeked out.

"The coast is clear," I whispered. "Let's go!"

Outside, the fresh air felt good, but I could still smell the alcohol on my breath, so I popped a peppermint Life Saver in my mouth.

Approximately halfway to the dance, the bourbon kicked in. Objects appeared farther away than they actually were, and I felt a little lightheaded. I also started laughing for no reason. When we arrived at the dance, I welcomed the opportunity to sit down. I felt like I was in a dream. The music, even "Good Vibrations," sounded blurry, and the band looked far away. I also felt much less inhibited, so I asked girls to dance who I would never have approached before.

On the way home, we had the misfortune of running into Killer Kelly, an older guy from the park's Night Shift. He was a big redheaded Irish kid known to be tough as nails. His reputation as a bully was well known, particularly when he was drunk, which was almost always. He stopped us and demanded money. His face was beet red, and he smelled like the inside of a beer can. When we told him we had no money, he took a swing at me. Luckily, I was able to dodge him, and he fell on his face. When he did, we ran like hell, knowing that if he'd connected, it would have been all over for us.

Following the Killer Kelly encounter and my severe hangover the next day, I decided to stick to acting and getting "Good Vibrations" from the song and good times, NOT from a bottle!

Chapter XX

One Last Look Back

Two days before Pete was to leave for boot camp, he and I took a trip to Brentwood on the Long Island Railroad. Pete had enlisted in the Marines through their "buddy plan," so he'd joined with Nick, a guy he'd met while working at Irving Trust. The plan guaranteed that he and Nick would be assigned to the same unit for basic training. While there were no guarantees after that, Pete figured that going through basic training with at least one familiar face was better than doing it with complete strangers.

Pete wanted to see Nick to double-check the necessary paperwork and finalize the location where they'd meet to get sworn in. Nick lived out in Brentwood, not far from Ralphie, Lisa, and Pete's uncle Eddie.

Nick picked us up at the train station in his Oldsmobile 442. The 442 had been introduced the year before and was fully loaded for racing with a four hundred-plus horsepower engine, four-speed stick transmission, and double-barrel carburetor. The dashboard had more dials on it than the cockpit of a plane. From the way Nick drove it, I thought that his time in the Marines might prove to be safer.

At Nick's house, we met his family and made small talk. Then we spent time with his father, who spoke about his days in the service. He was enormously proud of Nick. Nick's mother, on the other hand, appeared anxious and sad. Upon meeting Pete, however, she perked up and gave him a big hug. But as the discussion about the service continued, she choked up and went into the kitchen. When she returned, she was composed, but her eyes were clearly red from crying.

Pete, Nick, and I then went to Nick's room, where Pete and Nick checked their paperwork and agreed on a meeting place at the induction center. Nick's room had all the trappings of suburban living. He had his own TV and stereo, a full assortment of music albums, neatly framed photos of his family, friends, and girlfriend, and an assortment of baseball and football trophies. On the door to his closet was a large poster of a Marine in dress blues holding a saber. "The Few, The Proud, The Marines" was written underneath. It was a far cry from the small, cramped bedroom I shared with my brother.

After leaving Nick's, Pete and I took a walk over to Lisa's house a few blocks away. Lisa and I were still going out and corresponded with each other up to three times a week. She sure wrote great letters, sometimes ten or twelve pages in length. In response, I wrote long ones back, finding it much easier to put thoughts and feelings in writing rather than to say them in person. In her latest letter, she had asked me if Pete would stop over so she and her family could wish him luck. It would also provide an opportunity for the two of us to see each other.

We stayed at Lisa's for an hour. Lisa's mother, Fran, was there along with Lisa's brother, Sal, and their little sister, Francine. Lisa's father, Sam, was still working his second job in the City and would not be home for several hours. When it was time for us to go, Fran and Lisa gave Pete a big hug and wished him all the best. Pete promised Lisa he would send her a picture of himself in his dress blues once it was available. I gave Lisa a kiss on the lips and promised to return in a few weeks. In between that time, our steady exchange of letters would continue.

We then headed over to see Pete's Uncle Eddie, Aunt Peggy, and his grandmother, who lived with them. The walk there took fifteen minutes, long enough for Pete to give me another pep talk on how I had made a smart move by going out with Lisa.

"I'll tell you, Dan, the girl is going to be a knockout! She already looks like she's dropping that baby fat. You'll see."

I hadn't noticed much weight loss, but I welcomed his words of encouragement. Almost a year had passed since Lisa and I had resumed going out, and I'd be starting college that September.

Patience, I told myself. Maybe it would all work out the way I had hoped!

When we arrived, there was a big hello from Eddie, Peggy, and Pete's grandmother. Eddie was Pete's mother's youngest brother, and we had been out here several times for christenings and birthdays. Eddie and Peggy had a large family—five kids and counting, because Peggy was expecting. The first time I ever visited was when Eddie and Peggy's youngest, Catherine, had been christened. The family had all treated me warmly, like I was one of their own, and I'd grown close to them. Following the greetings, we settled down for a full-course dinner sprinkled with lots of talk about Pete going into the service. By now, I had memorized most of the details and sometimes responded to the questions as though I were the one going away rather than Pete.

Following coffee and desert, it was time for us to leave. The ride home on the railroad and subway would take close to two-and-a-half hours, and we wanted to get an early start. Pete received more good wishes and intentions to pray for him. His aunt and grandmother were both deeply religious and assured him he'd be in their daily prayers. They also reminded me that I shouldn't be a stranger and to make sure that I stopped over when I came out to see Lisa. Then Eddie gave us a lift to the train station.

We all crowded into the front seat of Eddie's station wagon as we waited for the train to arrive. During our wait, Eddie shared a few stories from his days in the Navy. By the nature of his stories, Pete and I both got the sense that Eddie was acknowledging that we had grown up. When the train pulled in, Eddie, Pete and I got out of the car. Eddie gave Pete an affectionate pat on the back followed by a strong handshake for both of us. Then Pete and I stepped up onto the train. Through the windows, we saw Eddie waving as the conductor bellowed, "All aboard!"

Then the train chugged out of the station.

We found seats facing each other near a window and settled in. The view was little more than blurred streetlights passing by in hypnotic fashion After a brief silence, we got around to discussing the day's events, with the conversation gradually shifting to speculation about what lay in store for us in the future.

My future, or at least the next seven years, seemed to be well scheduled. A five-year electrical engineering program at City College followed by the two years I'd probably spend in the service. Beyond that, who knew? Maybe I'd marry Lisa and apply for astronaut training.

For Pete, it was clear what he'd be doing for the next two years. Beyond that, maybe he'd head back to the bank and finish college at night. In some ways, I envied him. After his two-year hitch in the service, he'd be free to pursue whatever he wanted. On the other hand, I felt like I had to wait seven years before I could get on with my life. At the age of sixteen, seven years seemed like another lifetime. I again found myself wishing I had that time machine.

Following the train and subway rides, we arrived at the Wycoff and Myrtle Avenue Station of the "L" line. Pete headed to his house and I headed to mine. He'd spend one more full day home with his family, and on the day after, Saturday, he'd leave for the service.

On Friday night, I headed over to Pete's house. He'd asked me to ride with him and his father when he left on Saturday morning. After all the stuff I had been through with Pete and his family, it seemed only natural that we all be together the night before he left. My parents understood and allowed me to sleep over.

That evening, we spent a lot of time just shooting the bull about all sorts of things: the block, the Bombers, the girls, the schemes, and the crowd in general. By now everyone had gone off in different directions, and for most of the past year, Pete and I had palled around like Butch Cassidy and the Sundance Kid. Now everything would be changing. While I had wished I could speed up the future, I also wished I could replay the past. The last four years had brought so many changes, and I was no longer that Boy Scout from years ago.

As we talked about the future, I told Pete that if I married Lisa, I wanted him to be the best man. Here I was, sixteen years old, already talking about getting married. Yet it all seemed so real. We both felt much older than our ages. Having followed the familiar pattern of discussing the past and then the future, the conversation shifted to the present—tonight. This would be the last of our marathon bull sessions for a while. I told him I'd be sure to write once I received his address. After my long-distance romance with Lisa, I felt I had become a prolific letter writer. I just had to figure out when I'd find the time to do it. I promised, however, that I would.

During our conversation, I felt totally in touch with my being, with who I was, where I was, and what I wanted to do with my life. I always felt that way on the block, but now the feeling was stronger than ever. After a while, the discussion faded into sleep, and before I realized it, Pete's father was nudging me on the shoulder.

"Danny, it's seven thirty. Time to get up."

Pete had to report to Fort Hamilton in Brooklyn at 1100 hours, or 11:00 a.m. Though the car ride there was only forty-five minutes, we wanted to get an early start, particularly in view of Steve's track record of getting lost. Despite the mere three or four hours' sleep we had gotten, I felt wide awake.

The atmosphere in the house was solemn. You could cut the air with a knife. In between the trips that Pete, Steve, and I made to the bathroom to wash up, Pete's mother could be heard sobbing in her bedroom and then from behind the bathroom door. Pete's sister, Margaret, and his brothers were all up as well, quietly munching cereal at the kitchen table with sleepy looks of confusion and sadness on their faces. There was no easy way for this morning to happen.

When we were almost ready to go, I told Pete I'd wait out on the stoop. I wanted to give him and his family some time alone together. Standing on the stoop near Pete's infamous bedroom window, I heard him kiss his younger sister and brothers goodbye and remind them to behave while he was away. He told young Stephen that if he received bad reports when he came home from basic training, he'd try out some hand-combat torture holds on him. As I listened to him, I laughed to myself. The old *Friday Night Wrestling* maneuver. I pictured the expression on Stephen's face. When Pete finished, his siblings, little Michael in particular, assured him they would behave.

Then I heard Pete's mother break down sobbing again.

"Peter, just be careful," she pleaded.

"I will, Mom, I will," he said in a whisper.

This was it.

There was no holding back.

As I leaned against the black cast-iron stair railing, I fought hard to hold back tears. I heard the door close and simultaneously saw Pete and his father approach the front door from within the narrow hallway.

First Pete, then Steve.

There was nothing to be said.

We silently headed toward Steve's green 1953 DeSoto, parked right in front of the house. Pete and Steve sat in the front, and I settled in the back with Pete's overnight bag beside me.

"You have everything you need?" Steve asked Pete in a fatherly tone of voice.

"Yeah, Dad, I think so." Pete responded.

Even if he had forgotten something, he probably wouldn't have returned inside to face his mother and the kids again.

Steve started the engine, and we quietly sat there as the car warmed up. Even though it was late August, Steve's car always needed to warm up so it wouldn't stall out.

"One of these days, I got to get this heap tuned up," Steve mumbled as if reading my thoughts.

A couple of minutes later, Steve pulled out.

We were on our way.

The trip to Fort Hamilton was quiet, the only sounds coming from the radio in the middle of the dashboard. After a brief news update, the weather reporter announced that it would be a hot day with a chance of thunderstorms later that evening. Then the latest popular song, "I'm A Believer" by The Monkees, played a few times, along with a barrage of commercials from Dennison's, a clothing store in New Jersey. We must have heard "Money Talks! Nobody Walks! At Dennison's!" a hundred times.

True to form, Steve wound up getting lost on one of his infamous shortcuts. He made a wrong turn and we found ourselves near Prospect Park. In some ways, getting lost proved to be a blessing; it distracted us from the purpose of the trip and killed time that might otherwise have been spent awkwardly waiting at the induction center.

After a few minutes of reviewing a map from my navigator's spot in the back, I helped correct our course, and we had a few laughs at Steve's expense.

A half hour later, we turned off the exit of the Belt Parkway leading into Fort Hamilton. At the front gate, a Marine guard directed us to the reception center where Pete was to report. As a result of our early departure and despite the mistaken shortcut, we still had fifteen minutes to kill before Pete had to leave.

We sat in Steve's car making small talk about the weather,

then performed a last-minute check to ensure that Pete had all the papers and other things he needed. Following the short eternity, the time to say goodbye had finally arrived.

I handed Pete his overnight bag.

"Send me your address once you get settled. I'll write you as soon as I can."

"Okay, buddy. Will do." He shook my hand while deliberately avoiding eye contact.

Then he and Steve got out of the car. I climbed out from the back and moved into the front while they walked a few yards ahead and then stopped, still within listening distance.

"Well, Pete, I guess this is it," Steve said, his voice beginning to crack. "Take care of yourself and make sure you let your mother and I know how you're doing once you get settled."

"Okay, Dad, I will," Pete said as they hugged.

After embracing his father for about thirty seconds, Pete picked up his bag and proceeded toward the induction center while Steve slowly backpedaled to the car. Halfway to the center, Pete turned and took one last look back with a slight wave. Steve and I returned the wave, then Pete turned and headed to the reception center, entering through its two large wooden doors.

Once inside the car, Steve could no longer hold back the tears. He put his head on the steering wheel and sobbed uncontrollably. I looked at him and then straight ahead through the windshield. There was nothing I could do or say. My eyes filled with huge tears, but I fought hard to hold them back, figuring it wouldn't help Steve if I also started crying.

After a few minutes, Steve composed himself, took out his hankie, and blew his nose. "It's hard to see your son go into the service," he said.

"I know," I said, not knowing what else to say to help the situation.

On the way back to Pete's house, Steve and I stopped for coffee and talked about which teams might wind up in the World Series. The stop gave Steve time to prepare himself for when he returned home. Pete's mother had been really broken up about his departure, and Steve would have to remain strong to support her.

When we arrived at the house, I declined Steve's offer to come in. This was a time for the family to spend together by themselves.

"Now, make sure you're not a stranger," Steve admonished, his voice coming back to full strength. "Come around for dinner. You're always welcome in our house."

"I will."

Then I headed home along the route that I had traveled so many times over the past four years. As I walked, I tried to sort out the feelings flooding me, especially those of tremendous loss and emptiness.

It felt like a special time in my life was coming to an end, even though I didn't want it to. After years of new adventures and good times, the crowd had moved off in different directions. Pete going into the service was the final chapter, and it felt like things would never ever be the same.

As it turned out, I was right.

They never were.

Chapter XXI

... And Now

Sometimes in the morning as I commute to work on the Long Island Railroad and gaze out the window, the passing houses and streetlights hypnotically transport me to earlier times, when Pete and I would travel out to Brentwood. On other occasions, when I'm driving near the old neighborhood, I find myself taking a detour to Woodbine Street.

Slowly I cruise down the old block, drinking in all the old memories along the way. The lumberyard fence is still there, and so is the old knitting mill doorway where we hit harmony. The houses, like old friends, show their age, their bricks slightly worn and their painted trim fading. As I proceed, I receive curious looks from the young kids to whom the block now belongs.

Their peering eyes seem to ask, Who is this stranger, and why is he taking so long to drive down our block?

At around midblock, my eyes scan the ground for the old stickball bases—faded signs of a bygone era. Slightly farther along, I pull over to the curb adjacent to the fire hydrant we once scaled.

I emerge from my car with an old broomstick in one hand and a brand-new Spaldeen in the other.

Then I walk toward the sewer cover that once served as

home plate.

I look up the block at the lumberyard fence, then focus on tossing up the ball and preparing to swing.

One bounce, two bounces, then…

SWOOSH.

On my very first swing, the bat hits the ball with a stinging sound. I follow its path as it launches into a steadily rising trajectory that triumphantly ends on a pile of lumber on the other side of the fence. It bounces once and disappears from sight. Suddenly I am lost in time and tempted to take a victory lap around the old bases.

Comments from the local kids snap me back to the present, and I immediately change my mind. Before turning back to my car, I hand the stickball bat to one of the kids, along with a second Spaldeen I'd brought as a spare. I smile at the kid, and he returns the smile in silence as he accepts my gifts. When I reach my car and open the door, I am filled with a huge sense of satisfaction. Finally, after so many years, the asterisk with which I lived can finally be erased! I also feel like I have passed on important souvenirs from my generation to the new one residing on the block.

I start my car and proceed underneath the old elm trees that seem to be leaning farther over from age. I pass Lisa's old house and then Timmy's. From the opposite side of the street, I expect to hear warning screams in broken English from M.C.'s grandfather. A few yards on stands the six-family house once occupied by Pete and the Twins.

As I pass them, I wonder if these houses remember me. And if they do, what might they now be thinking?

Finally, I come to the stop sign at the Irving Avenue end of the block, and I'm strongly tempted to "peel out and lay rubber." A smile crosses my face as I recall the triumphant victory over the infamous Chevy 409 creep.

Then I pause and take a look in my rearview mirror. I see the kids on the block taking swings at the Spaldeen with their new stickball bat. In that moment, I expect to see M.C., Timmy, Lisa, the Twins, and Pete come barreling onto the block.

A few seconds pass that feel like an eternity, then a driver behind me beeps. I steal one final look in the rearview mirror and step on the gas.

It's time to move on.

Acknowledgments

My deepest appreciation to all those who supported me throughout the process of first thinking about this book and then making it a reality.

Special thanks to my good friend John Kastan, my wonderful daughter-in-law, Krista Holford, and Anne McAneny for their editing assistance during the numerous years it took to bring this book to reality.

Grateful appreciation to Susan Walsh McLean, whose enormous artistic talent actualized the vision I had for the book's cover from its early days of inception.

Finally, many thanks to Veronica Perretti and Amy DeFilippi for their terrific work in creating the website for Street Corner Universe.

Note: If you enjoyed this book and would like to leave a review on the site of your choice, I would very much appreciate your time and effort. My dream is for as many people as possible to realize that they too have their own street corner universes to enjoy or recall. Thank you all.   –Don

About the Author

Don Holford was born and raised in Brooklyn, New York. He and his wife, Laraine, currently reside in New Jersey. Together they share four children, including Jonathan, Don's son from his first marriage, and Laraine's children with her late husband: Joe, Amy, and Peter. They also celebrate five amazing grandchildren, who keep them in step with life's seasons.

When Don's not working or writing, you'll find him golfing, reading historical novels, or running 5K and five-mile races at the Jersey Shore. He is especially proud of having completed the New York City Marathon three times.

With the publication of *Street Corner Universe*, Don has fulfilled a longtime dream of sharing an important time in his life, including the friends with whom he shared it.

A product of New York City's public school system, including Brooklyn Tech, Don went on to attain multiple master's degrees and has held senior management positions throughout New York City in both government and nonprofit organizations. He is currently the President and CEO of his own management consulting firm.

Over the years, Don has embraced the life view that if one argues for their limitations, they get to keep them, but if one argues for their possibilities, they get to create them. He has especially enjoyed quality time with his sons, daughter, daughters-in-law, and grandchildren, imparting street corner wisdom on the choice of stickball bats, Spaldeens, and baseball gloves.

Having now told the story of *Street Corner Universe*, Don is hard at work on its sequel, tentatively titled *Street Corner Universe: New Explorations.*

Don would love to hear readers' recollections of their own adolescent adventures. Connect with him on social media, and be sure to check out his website, where you can share fun experiences from your teen years and sign up to receive alerts when the new book is released.

Website: StreetCornerUniverse.com

Facebook Fan Page: Street Corner Universe
(*Facebook.com/StreetCornerUniverse*)

Instagram: StreetCornerUniverse
(Instagram.com/StreetCornerUniverse)

Printed in Great Britain
by Amazon

56623076R00137